EDUCATED
PERSON'S
Thumbnail
Introduction
TO THE
Bible

THE EDUCATED PERSON'S

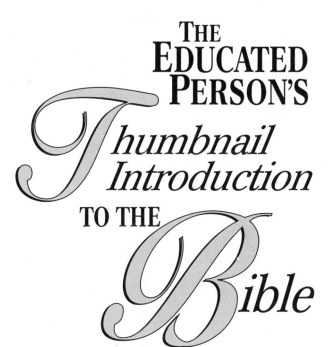

Thumbnail Introduction

TO THE

Bible

Lowell K. Handy

Chalice Press

St. Louis, Missouri

Biblical quotations, unless otherwise noted, are from the *New Revised Standard Version Bible*, copyright 1989, Division of Christian Education of the National Council of the Churches of Christ in the USA. Used by permission.

Cover and interior design: Lynne Condellone

10 9 8 7 6 5 4 3 2   98 99 00 01 02

Library of Congress Cataloging–in–Publication Data

Handy, Lowell K., 1949–
    The educated person's thumbnail introduction to the Bible / Lowell K. Handy
        p.   cm.
    Includes bibliographical references
    ISBN 0-8272-0810-3
    1. Bible—Introductions.   I. Title
BS475.2.H244   1997   97-6401
220.6'1 —dc21   CIP

Printed in the United States of America

For the members of
First Christian Church
Fort Dodge, Iowa

as we start our second century
1896–

$\mathcal{T}$ABLE OF CONTENTS

$\mathcal{I}$NTRODUCTION

I have been part of and been leader of a number of church Bible studies, as well as having taught Sunday school. Some things about the Bible as the central book of the church never seemed to come up in the texts used. Bible study volumes usually deal with specific Bible topics, individual books of the Bible, or ways one can use the Bible in one's own life. These are all useful approaches, but they almost always assume that the Bible is one book, the same for everyone who would be looking at scripture, and that is not the case throughout Christianity, let alone Judaism. This volume was designed to be used as a change from normal Bible study texts and to give the participants some insight into the Bible in the larger religious community that uses "the Bible." The varieties of Bibles and interpretations of the sacred texts in the world might help to locate individual Bible study groups (and individuals) in the history and theology of the Christian, Jewish, and even Muslim traditions.

The intention was to introduce on a simple level some of the breadth and depth of Bible use in the Western religious traditions. To do this it is necessary to acknowledge scholarship in Jewish and Muslim circles as well as Christian, for these three religious traditions owe much understanding of their sacred books to each other. Within Christianity itself there are numerous manners of reading the Bible, and, indeed, numerous Bibles to read. An ecumenical approach has been attempted, such that an effort has been made to present each tradition as much on its own terms as possible.

For some congregations (and for some members) Bible interpretations that differ from their own are, by definition, wrong. This volume is not an attempt to change anyone's mind about how he or she prefers to read the Bible, but only to allow the reader to glimpse the manner in which others read the same Bible and come up with different meanings. Common ground among all Bible readers is impossible (as should become clear in the course of reading this volume), but understanding how others read the text should be possible and, I think, both interesting and beneficial.

The chapters are designed to deal with one topic individually on its own; however, the content of the first chapter is assumed by the later chapters and the section on reading the chapter and verse numbers in chapter 4 is presumed throughout. Otherwise, the group may pick out chapters to use and skip others. I have included thirteen chapters, since that would provide one chapter a week for a quarter of a year. Aspects of the Bible not usually dealt with and often ignored or unknown at the congregational level form the common thread for the text.

There are not only chapters that deal with the variety of Jewish, Orthodox Christian, Roman Catholic, and Protestant Bibles and Bible interpretation, but also on the questions related to translations; where the chapter and verse numbers came from (and why they are *not* part of the Bible itself); problems currently being fought over among Bible scholars; and a final chapter on some names that people interested in the Bible ought to have at least heard.

I hope that the volume will help people who use the Bible understand others who also use the Bible. It is a little contribution to ecumenical understanding in a multicultural world, but one I think we can all make.

As for Bibles to be used in the study, any Bible you happen to have at hand would be fine. It is better to study Bibles with a rich assortment to look at, however. If there is interest, I would recommend rounding up for the sessions as many of the following as reasonable:

Revised Standard Version (American Protestant)
New Revised Standard Version with Apocrypha
   (update of RSV)

King James Version (the official Anglican Reformation
    translation)
New King James Version (update of the KJV)
Tanak—The Holy Scriptures (Jewish Publication Society)
    [Jewish]
New American Bible (popular Catholic translation)
Jerusalem Bible (liturgical Catholic translation)
New International Version (American Protestant)
New English Bible (official modern Anglican translation)
Revised New English Bible (update of NEB)
Good News Bible (Bible in common American English)

If members of the study group read languages other than English,
Bibles in those languages should be brought and compared.

At the end of the chapters I have listed some readings that I
used to write the chapter or that would supply interested persons
with further sources to study. Books can often be obtained through
interlibrary loan; journal articles are more difficult. However, some
resource works have been useful throughout, so I list them here.

Encyclopedias and Dictionaries

The New Catholic Encyclopedia and *Encyclopaedia Judaica* are
two of the finest religious reference tools for research on anyone
from these two traditions. For short entries on persons and movements, the one-volume *The Oxford Dictionary of the Christian Church*,
2nd ed., edited by F. L. Cross and E. A. Livingstone (London: Oxford University, 1974) is exceptional. For Bible materials the stan-
dards: *The Interpreter's Dictionary of the Bible,* 5 vols. (Nashville:
Abingdon, 1962, 1976) and *The Anchor Bible Dictionary,* 6 vols.
(New York: Doubleday, 1992) provide lengthy articles on many
topics covered here.

Introductions

A very readable introduction to the Bible is currently available
in Christian E. Hauer and William A. Young, *An Introduction to the
Bible: A Journey into Three Worlds,* 3rd ed. (Englewood Cliffs, N.J.:
Prentice Hall, 1994). For introductions that deal extensively with
approaches to the text the following are useful: Otto Eissfeldt, *The
Old Testament: An Introduction* (New York: Harper and Row, 1965)
[old and difficult reading, but still a fine introduction to the Higher
Critical study of the First Testament]; Stephen Bigger, ed., *Creating*

the Old Testament: The Emergence of the Hebrew Bible (Oxford: Basil Blackwell, 1989) [more readable, but still scholarly]; Werner Georg Kümmel, *Introduction to the New Testament,* revised ed. (Nashville: Abingdon, 1975) [old and dense reading]; Russell Pregeant, *Engaging the New Testament: An Interdisciplinary Introduction* (Minneapolis: Augsburg/Fortress, 1994) [covers current approaches well].

Bible Histories
The standard English history of the Bible and its interpretation remains *The Cambridge History of the Bible,* 3 vols. (Cambridge: Cambridge University Press, 1963, 1969, 1970). A much more thorough history is provided in the French series *Bible de tous les temps,* 8 vols. (Paris: Bauchesne, 1984-1989).

THERE ARE BIBLES

WHEN SOMEONE WALKS INTO A BOOKSTORE AND ASKS FOR A BIBLE, the customer usually has an idea that what is desired is a single volume, the title of which designates a book understood to be the same by everyone. "The Bible," however, is a different volume to different religious groups that share a similar history. This is not just a distinction between the Jewish Bible and the Christian Bible, but a series of different, but related, sacred texts for members within these two traditions as well as between them.

The Bible is a collection of several books that in today's world of bound volumes usually appears in the hands of members of religious communities as a single book. Originally, all the separate "books" of the Bible were distinct works. Generally speaking, Old Testament works appeared early in their existence as their own scrolls while New Testament manuscripts were written in codices (a forerunner of modern books) or as individual letters (later copied together into collections).

The independent works that were determined to be authoritative in a special sense for the religious tradition came to form the *canon* of the tradition. *Canon* means "list"; a word that came to English from a Greek word borrowed from the Semitic word for "reed," an item used for measuring objects. The word is now used for authoritative lists of many different items; the Catholic Church has an official canon of saints, and academic fields have canons of texts necessary for understanding particular areas of study. In the case of Holy Scripture, the canon refers to the official list of books that are accepted by the religious community as authoritative to bear the word of God.

The canon for scripture is not the same for all people who use the biblical books in the Jewish and Christian traditions. As religious groups divided from each other throughout the history of Judaism and Christianity, they determined for themselves which of the books held by the tradition were to be authoritative for their own faith. Today there are a number of canons in use, more than can be considered here; however, the following examples of Bibles used in the contemporary religious world should demonstrate something of the variety among the various biblical canons.

Samaritan Pentateuch

The smallest Bible in use in the modern world is that of the Samaritans. Though a small religious community, they continue to thrive in the area of ancient Samaria, now part of the West Bank of modern Israel. At the time when Jews and Samaritans still acknowledged their religious relations with each other (the Persian Period, 539–331 B.C.E. perhaps extending into the early Seleucid Period, 331–167 B.C.E.) both communities held as sacred texts only five scrolls. These works now form the first five books of all Jewish and Christian Bibles but form the entire Bible of the Samaritans, who never added additional writings to their canon. The term "Pentateuch," used for this canon, simply means "five books" and is used in modern biblical discussion to refer to the first five books of the Bible, no matter which Bible is under discussion.

The canon of authoritative scripture for a Samaritan, therefore, consists of:

Genesis	Numbers
Exodus	Deuteronomy
Leviticus	

It is true that there are several differences in the content of these books from that of the Jewish or Christian books of the same name, but the differences are, for the most part, minor. There is no question that the Samaritans and the Jews, before their parting, held the same Pentateuch as sacred.

Jewish Tanak

The Jewish Bible consists of three parts. The common name given to the collection is an anagram of the Hebrew names for the three sections: Tanak = Torah, Nebi'im, and Ketubim (pronounced: tora, neviim, and kethuvim). Unlike the Samaritan Pentateuch, or Roman Catholic or Protestant canons, the three divisions of the Jewish Bible have different levels of authority.

The first section consists of the same five books as the Samaritan Pentateuch; however, in Jewish Bibles this section is called the Torah. "Torah" is often translated by Christians as "law," but the word actually means "instruction" and contains much more than legal material. Throughout Jewish history the Torah has always been the most important section of the Bible. Like the Samaritan Pentateuch, it consists of Genesis, Exodus, Leviticus, Numbers, and Deuteronomy.

The second section of the Tanak is called "Prophets" (*Nebi'im*). These books relate the stories and proclamations of those who spoke the words of God. In the published editions of Jewish canon this section is divided into two parts: the Former Prophets and the Latter Prophets. The Former Prophets consist of four books:

Joshua	Samuel
Judges	Kings

When the scrolls of Samuel and Kings were converted to Codices (an early forerunner of books), it was discovered that the pages were too many for the codex to keep from breaking apart, so each of the two books was divided into two parts, giving modern Bibles in both Jewish and Christian canons four instead of two books: First Samuel, Second Samuel, First Kings, Second Kings. The Latter Prophets consist of four books from the four scrolls containing the prophecies ascribed to particular prophets. These books are divided into two parts:

Major Prophets:	Minor Prophets:
Isaiah	The Twelve
Jeremiah	
Ezekiel	

The scroll of "The Twelve" consists of the twelve minor prophets, whose individual sections of this scroll tend to be printed as individual books in Jewish Bibles, as they are in Christian Bibles.

The order of the prophets in the scroll of The Twelve is not set; the only requirement is that Malachi should be the last prophet in the series (for Malachi is understood in Jewish tradition to have been the last genuine prophet).

The third section is called "Writings" (Ketubim) and consists of a variety of literary material. These texts carry the least authority of the books in the Tanak, and the order of their printing within the section varies from Bible to Bible. It is traditional to end the Tanak with Chronicles (another scroll divided into two books when transferred to codex). Usually the five scrolls read in their entirety on set holy days are printed together and referred to as "the Five Scrolls": Song of Songs, Ruth, Lamentations, Ecclesiastes, and Esther. The other books accepted in the canon of Jewish biblical writings are Psalms, Proverbs, Job, Daniel, Ezra, and Nehemiah; there is no definite order required for their placement in scripture.

While these books form the canon of the Jewish Bible, the notion of canon in Jewish tradition extends beyond the Bible proper. The Talmud, which appears in both a Babylonian and Palestinian edition, is a series of sixty-three tractates (individual books) providing the authoritative interpretations for reading the Tanak, especially the Torah. These works are also treated by the Jewish scholarly community as revealed by God and authoritative. However, for the Tanak the Talmud is important because it is the discussions of the rabbis recorded therein that determined the accepted books of the Jewish Bible proper.

Roman Catholic Bible

For the majority of Christians the canon is that of the Roman Catholic Church. This canon was determined originally at the North African Council held in Carthage, 397 C.E., and "closed" at the Council of Trent, 1546 C.E. The African Council effectively determined the church's collection of additional books now called the New Testament. However, the books that were decided to belong to the Old Testament have been debated from that time forward throughout Christendom.

Because the early church spoke, read, and wrote Greek, the canon that was determined to be authoritative for Christians was the Greek canon used by the Jewish community in Alexandria, Egypt. The Jewish population of Alexandria had translated its Bible into the language of its own current culture and, while containing the Torah and the Prophets, it held a larger number of Writings as authoritative than did the Jewish communities of Mesopotamia and Palestine, which were the religious communities that had determined the extent of the Jewish canon just described as the Tanak. The Old Testament for the Catholic Church therefore consists of a larger number of books than does the modern Jewish Bible. As with all Christian Bibles, the Torah and the Prophets are included as used in the Jewish communities that formed the basis for the early church. However, the Writings section was determined to be longer in Christianity, a process that was being decided in Jewish and Christian communities simultaneously in the first three centuries of the Common Era. The canon accepted by the Roman Catholic Church for the Old Testament was understood as having one level of authority and is not formally divided into sections. The books of the Catholic Old Testament in their usual bound order are:

Genesis	Tobit
Exodus	Judith
Leviticus	Esther
Numbers	First Maccabees
Deuteronomy	Second Maccabees
Joshua	Job
Judges	Psalms
Ruth	Proverbs
First Samuel	Ecclesiastes
(also called First Kings)	Song of Songs
Second Samuel	Wisdom of Solomon
(also called Second Kings)	Ecclesiasticus
First Kings	Isaiah
(also called Third Kings)	Jeremiah
Second Kings	Lamentations
(also called Fourth Kings)	Baruch
First Chronicles	Ezekiel
(also called First	Daniel
Paralipomenon)	Hosea
Second Chronicles	Joel
(also called Second	Amos
Paralipomenon)	Obadiah
Ezra	Jonah
(also called First Esdras)	Micah
Nehemiah	Nahum
(also called Second Esdras)	Habakkuk

Zephaniah   Zechariah
Haggai   Malachi

The Catholic canon includes a rewritten, longer Esther, and a lengthy prayer made by the three friends in the fiery furnace as well as three additional stories in Daniel that make the books different from those appearing in the Jewish Tanak.

The New Testament books determined for the Catholic canon have, with two exceptions, been accepted as the New Testament canon throughout Christianity worldwide. Having had a large collection of texts to choose from, including such widely popular early Christian literature as the Diatesseron (a Gospel by Tatian), the Epistle of Barnabas, the Apocalypse of Peter, the Shepherd of Hermas, and numerous other works used for worship and study in the early churches, the Bishops who had gathered for the North African Council, held in Carthage, chose to form their authoritative Christian canon around four gospels, the letters of Paul, and a collection of catholic letters (letters written to be circulated among the churches). To these was added the book of the Acts of the Apostles and one apocalypse (not without debate and not without dissension). The New Testament canon in its usual modern western church order appears as follows:

Matthew   First Timothy
Mark   Second Timothy
Luke   Titus
John   Philemon
Acts of the Apostles   Hebrews
Romans   James
First Corinthians   First Peter
Second Corinthians   Second Peter
Galatians   First John
Ephesians   Second John
Philippians   Third John
Colossians   Jude
First Thessalonians   Revelation to John
Second Thessalonians

Some very early church collections of books followed the Book of Acts with the catholic epistles (James through Jude above) and then placed those letters ascribed to Paul after them. It is interesting to note that the order in which the gospels are now placed in the New

Testament was not determined until the Middle Ages and the order of the Pauline correspondence is from longest (Romans) to shortest (Philemon), an ordering system also used in Islam for the books of the Qur'an. Hebrews, an early church sermon, was early ascribed to Paul, but most early Christian scholars denied it was of Pauline authorship; it therefore appears after the letters deemed by the council to have been genuinely Pauline, meaning either by Paul himself or by an immediate associate. (As for the Pastorals, First and Second Timothy and Titus, they were doubted by some to have been by Paul from the earliest records of their existence, so the current debates on their authorship began, in fact, as soon as they were collected by the early church.)

Many Roman Catholic Bibles also include the books of the Catholic Apocrypha. The Catholic Apocrypha consists of works that appeared in Septuagint (Greek) manuscripts of the Bible but were not declared canonical at the North African Council in Carthage. These books are: First Esdras (also called Third Esdras), Second Esdras (also called Fourth Esdras), The Prayer of Manasseh, and Psalm 151. These books are not to be confused with the Protestant Apocrypha, which consists solely of books canonical within the Roman Catholic Bible but not in Protestant Bibles. It was common until after the Second Vatican Council to include the Catholic Apocryphal books of First and Second Esdras in bound Catholic Bibles; however, the status of the two books as less than canonical has always been maintained.

Greek Orthodox Bible

Though the Septuagint was the Greek translation used by the Jewish community in Alexandria and was the basis of the Christian Old Testament, not all of the books that appear in the collections of this translation (for there were several differences even in the canons represented in the Greek-speaking Jewish Alexandrian community) were accepted by the Roman Catholic Church. Most of the remaining books of the Alexandrian Jewish canon have been retained in the longer canon of the Greek Orthodox Church. Though participants in the African Council that set the authoritative canon for church discussions, the Greek Bishops were not, obviously, participants at the Council of Trent that closed the Roman Catholic canon. This means that the Greek Orthodox Church still retains the "open" canon interpretation of the exact extent of scripture. The New Testament is that of the Carthage Council, but the Old Testament remains fluid among Greek Orthodox Church congregations.

The modern Greek Orthodox churches do not use the Greek Septuagint language, but either a Greek text as developed within Greece itself and used throughout the history of the Byzantine Empire, or a modern Greek translation. As for the canon, some congregations accept as authoritative the Old Testament essentially as it appeared in the Septuagint. This means that for some Greek communities the Old Testament contains all the books of the Roman Catholic Bible (though Baruch is usually not considered canonical in Orthodox churches) as well as the following, all coming from Septuagint manuscript tradition (this from the list approved by the Holy Synod of the Greek Orthodox Church):

First Esdras
    (also known as Third Ezra [not Ezra])
Prayer of Manasseh
Third Maccabees
Fourth Maccabees
Psalm 151
    (appearing as the last psalm in the Book of Psalms)

Other Greek Orthodox congregations have chosen to treat as canonical only the books described by Gregory the Theologian (traditionally in the western church called Gregory Nazianzus, 329–389 C.E.) in a list he compiled just prior to the African Council. His Old Testament canon is that of the Jewish Tanak with two exceptions: Lamentations is not treated as a separate book but is appended within Jeremiah, and the book of Esther is not included as a canonical work at all.

Coptic Orthodox Church Bible

The church took early root in Egypt, and the Coptic Orthodox Church remains roughly 10 percent of the Egyptian population after over a thousand years of Islamic rule. The canon of the Copts is very close to that of the Roman Catholic Church, but with four major differences. In the Old Testament the Book of Psalms contains the 151st Psalm, as do some Greek Orthodox canons. In the Eastern Orthodox churches the 151st Psalm may or may not appear in the official Book of Psalms; or, as in the Coptic Bibles (as with the Greek Orthodox), the Book of Psalms may contain the 151st in some editions and not contain it in others, both versions of the Psalms being accepted as canonical. (This is also true of the psalms numbered 151–155 that appear in the East Syriac canonical Book of Psalms; the Dead Sea scrolls have shown, however, that these "extra" psalms were already in use by the first century B.C.E.) In addition to the rest of the books found in the Catholic Bible, the Coptic Old Testament contains Third Maccabees, following Second Maccabees.

The Coptic New Testament is the sole modern Christian canon with more books than the Catholic Church's New Testament. Following the Revelation to John is the book Clement, which contains the two existing "letters" (the second is a sermon) ascribed to Bishop Clement of Rome in one biblical book. The Coptic New Testament officially ends with the Apostolic Constitutions, a collection originally of eight books regarding the management of the early church, here taken as a single New Testament book.

Ethiopic Orthodox Church
The longest canon within the Christian world is that of the Ethiopic Orthodox Church. The church in Ethiopia traces its own history to the Ethiopian eunuch of Acts 8:26–39, though archaeological evidence in Ethiopia can confirm a Christian presence only from the fourth century. Having been cut off from both Eastern and Western Christian traditions with the rise of Islam, the Ethiopian Orthodox Church developed many independent traditions, including its own extended canon and its own interpretive methodology. There are, in fact, two recognized canons, one called "Wider" and one "Narrower"; the latter is the one that corresponds to the Bible among other Christian communities and is in itself the largest canon in the Jewish-Christian biblical tradition.

The Old Testament contains all the books of the Roman Catholic Church, plus a number of books found in other Eastern Orthodox canons, as well as two books found only in the Ethiopian Bible (Jubilees and Enoch). The order of the books in the Bible are unique to Ethiopian Bibles, but for purposes here the canon itself is of interest. Those books in the Ethiopian Old Testament, not found in the Catholic canon, are as follows:

Enoch
Third Ezra
(First Esdras in Greek Orthodox longer canons)
Fourth Ezra
(also called Second Esdras [not Nehemiah])

Third Maccabees
Psalm 151
    (appearing as the last psalm in the Book of Psalms)
Prayer of Manasseh
    (appended to Second Chronicles)
Jubilees

The New Testament of the Ethiopic Orthodox Church conforms to that of the Roman Catholic.

Protestant Bible

The Bible as it appears among the Protestant churches is a hybrid of traditions. Reform leaders, like Martin Luther and John Calvin, wished Bibles capable of being read by the laity and turned to translations from the Greek New Testament and the Hebrew Old Testament. Arguing that the true Bible of the early church was the Jewish Bible used by the synagogues of the reformers' own day, the Protestants translated the Tanak as their Old Testament. In this manner they removed from the official Protestant canon the works of the Alexandrian canon that had been accepted by the church Bishops at Carthage in 397 C.E. The books that appeared in the official Catholic Old Testament but did not appear in the Protestant canon were called the Apocrypha (literally: hidden) by the Protestants and sometimes have been published as an appendix to their Bibles as works which might also be read to one's advantage. The Catholic Church, at the Council of Trent, gave the name "Deuterocanon" (literally: second list) to the collection of books that is called by the Protestants the "Apocrypha" and declared them as authoritative and to be in no way treated as inferior to the rest of the canon.

The New Testament of the Protestant Bible simply retained the New Testament of the Catholic Bible. There are books of the New Testament with which the reformers were unhappy, but being unaware of any authority for removing any books of the New Testament canon, Luther was forced to retain Revelation, which he did not like, and James, which he despised. Of course, had he only known that there was (and still is) a New Testament canon that does not include Revelation or James (or Second and Third John, Second Peter, or Jude) Luther undoubtedly would have removed the offending books from the Lutheran canon. It is the East Syriac Orthodox Church that has the short New Testament canon, though they have added the remaining books to their modern Bible as a less authoritative section of texts (producing a two-part New Testament with different levels of authority) just to have available in their bound Bible all the volumes treated as New Testament canon by the vast majority of the rest of the church.

Questions for Reflection and Discussion

1. How many in the group were even aware that there was diversity among Christian denominations' canons?

2. Does it make any difference that there are so many different Bibles?

3. Jewish canon is divided into books that are more and less authoritative; does your community do this without actually dividing out the books in the Bible itself?

4. Some early Christian scholars referred to the Christian Bible (meaning the Old and New Testaments) as the "Prophets and the Apostles." What might that say about how they saw the collection in their Bible?

5. What would be the significance for the authority of the books of the Bible in use in one's own religious community if the Bible were the Samaritan Pentateuch, or the Ethiopian Orthodox canon?

Bibliographical Note

Further information about Christian canons may be found in an excellent article by Hans Peter Rüger, "The Extent of the Old Testament Canon," *The Bible Translator* 40 No. 3 (July 1989) pp. 301–308, to which this chapter owes its sections on the Coptic, Ethiopian, East Syriac, and part of the Greek Orthodox modern canons. For those interested in reading the canonical books of the rest of the Jewish-Christian traditions, the Deuterocanon along with a select group of other canonical books appears in the Apocrypha section of the *New Revised Standard Version with Apocrypha* (New York: Oxford University Press, 1989). All works now treated as canonical in the Hebrew/Old Testament biblical tradition with the exception of First and Second Esdras, may be found, along with dozens of related, but not canonical, texts in English translation in the two volume set edited by James H. Charlesworth, *The Old Testament Pseudepigrapha*, 2 vols. (Garden City, N.Y.: Doubleday, 1983, 1985). Jacob M. Myers, *I & II Esdras*, Anchor Bible 42 (Garden City, N.Y.: Doubleday, 1974), is a translation with very readable commentary on the two books of Esdras. The letters attributed to Clement are found in standard collections of the Apostolic Fathers of the Church, including: Kirsopp Lake, ed., *The Apostolic Fathers*, Loeb Classical Library (Cambridge, Md.: Harvard University Press. London: William Heinemann, 1913), or C. C. Richardson, *Early Christian Fathers*, Library of Christian Classics (Philadelphia: Westminster, 1953). A decidedly outdated, but available, English translation of the Apostolic Constitutions by James Donaldson appears as *Ante-Nicene Christian Library*, vol. 17, pt. 2 (Edinburgh: T. & T. Clark, 1870).

CANONS OF THE BIBLE

FIVE EXAMPLES
(ON THE FOLLOWING TWO PAGES)

Samaritan	Tanak	Catholic	Greek Orthodox	Ethiopian Orthodox
Pentateuch	Jewish canon	Canon	Long canon	Narrower canon
Genesis	*Torah*	Genesis	Genesis	Genesis
Exodus	Genesis	Exodus	Exodus	Exodus
Leviticus	Exodus	Leviticus	Leviticus	Leviticus
Numbers	Leviticus	Numbers	Numbers	Numbers
Deuteronomy	Numbers	Deuteronomy	Deuteronomy	Deuteronomy
	Deuteronomy	Joshua	Joshua	Enoch
	Prophets	Judges	Judges	Jubilees
	Former Prophets	Ruth	Ruth	Joshua
	Joshua	I Samuel	I Samuel	Judges
	Judges	II Samuel	II Samuel	Ruth
	Samuel	I Kings	I Kings	I Samuel
	Kings	II Kings	II Kings	II Samuel
	Latter Prophets	I Chronicles	I Chronicles	I Kings
	Isaiah	II Chronicles	II Chronicles	II Kings
	Jeremiah	Ezra	Prayer of Manasseh*	I Chronicles
	Ezekiel	Nehemiah	I Esdras*	II Chronicles
	The Twelve	Tobit	Ezra	Prayer of Manasseh
	Writings	Judith	Nehemiah	Ezra
	Psalms	Esther	Tobit*	Nehemiah
	Proverbs	I Maccabees	Judith*	3rd Ezra
	Job	II Maccabees	Esther*	4th Ezra
	Song of Songs	Job	I Maccabees*	Tobit
	Ruth	Psalms	II Maccabees*	Judith
	Lamentations			

Ecclesiastes	Proverbs	III Maccabees*	Esther
Esther (Hebrew)	Ecclesiastes	IV Maccabees*	I Maccabees
Daniel (Hebrew)	Song of Songs	Job	II Maccabees
Ezra	Wisdom of Solomon	Psalms (+151*)	III Maccabees
Nehemiah	Ecclesiasticus	Proverbs	Job
Chronicles	Isaiah	Ecclesiastes	Psalms (+151)
	Jeremiah	Song of Songs	Proverbs (=Prov 1–24)
	Lamentations	Wisdom of Solomon*	Tägsas (=Prov 25–31)
	Baruch °	Ecclesiasticus*	Wisdom of Solomon
	Ezekiel	Isaiah	Ecclesiastes
	Daniel	Jeremiah	Song of Songs
	Hosea	Lamentations ^	Ecclesiasticus
	Joel	Ezekiel	Isaiah
	Amos	Daniel•	Jeremiah
	Obadiah	Hosea	Baruch °
	Jonah	Amos	Lamentations
	Micah	Micah	Ezekiel
	Nahum	Joel	Daniel
	Habakkuk	Obadiah	Hosea
	Zephaniah	Jonah	Amos
	Haggai	Nahum	Micah
	Zechariah	Habakkuk	Joel
	Malachi	Zephaniah	Obadiah
		Haggai	Jonah
		Zechariah	Nahum
		Malachi	Habakkuk
			Zephaniah
			Haggai
			Zechariah
			Malachi

* Not in shorter Greek canon

° Includes the Letter of Jeremiah which appears in some canons as a separate book

• Shorter Greek canon uses Hebrew text

^ Shorter Greek canon includes as the final chapters of Jeremiah

*italics signify divisions **not** books*

Ethiopian Orthodox canon from: Hans Peter Rüger, "The Extent of the Old Testament Canon," *The Bible Translator* 40 (1989), pp. 301-308 (allowance made for typographical loss of a line of manuscript in the article list).

WHERE DID THESE $\mathcal{B}$OOKS COME FROM?

THE BOOKS OF THE BIBLE APPEARED OVER A LONG PERIOD. IN CHRISTIAN Bibles there is a division between Old and New Testaments; however, the actual writing of these books overlap slightly in time. The books of the Jewish Tanak (=Protestant Old Testament) were all composed prior to the time of the early church, in a span covering about 400 years, from the Babylonian exile to the Maccabean Revolt (587–164 B.C.E.). Traditions extending backward to the origins of the states of Judah and Israel are incorporated into the biblical books, but the canonical texts were products of the Second Temple Period. As for the New Testament, its books were written within one century (at the longest), beginning with Paul's first letter to the Thessalonians and ending with Second Peter (50–120? C.E.). The early Christian literature was heavily dependent on the "Torah and the Prophets" for its understanding of Jesus and the theology of the Christian movement.

A general outline of the production of the books of the Bible follows. For the vast majority of biblical books there is no known author. Traditions within the Jewish and Christian literatures have attached names to the various works, but only a few texts have known authors. The attestation of the writing of the Torah to Moses, along with Jeremiah as the author of Kings and Lamentations, and Samuel as the author of Samuel, and so forth, was the notion of rabbis centuries after the texts had been composed. At the same time, the second-century Christians attached names from their earliest writings to those same writings as authors; so, for example, we do not know who wrote any of the four canonical gospels, but we do know to whom the late second century-church decided to ascribe them.

Hebrew Bible and Old Testament Origins

Jewish traditional teaching has held that the Tanak was delivered to Moses on Sinai, but that he wrote only the Torah; the other books were supposed to have been written down by those who had learned them through the tradition of the "oral law" passed down from one generation to another. Christian traditions have usually accepted the Jewish notion of Moses as author of the Torah, but assume a divine inspiration for the rest of the books of the canon, believing each to have been first revealed at the time of the book's writing. Most Christians believe in this inspired writing of the Bible; however, many Western Christian communities believe in the human origin of texts that bear authoritative divine content. This section provides an abbreviated outline of the origins of the books of the Bible.

Those Who Wrote the Books of the Old Testament

Literacy in the ancient world was uncommon. Not only did the general populace usually not know how to read or write; neither did most of the rulers in the great empires. Reading and writing was a profession left, for the most part, to the scribes, who made good livings by their competence in literary, mathematical, and economic skills. All of the books of the Tanak were written by scribes, mostly employed either in the palace or temple bureaucracies, though Baruch appears to have been a private scribe in the employ of Jeremiah.

The majority of scribes were male, though some female scribes are known to have existed; they were usually children of families of some importance, who had been sent from an early age to scribal school where they studied not only reading and writing, but also mathematics, political science, proper court behavior, and the current visions of the world, both natural and social. A successful scribe could expect a good life with good pay and relatively light work (at least when compared to the rest of their contemporaries). There was status in being a scribe, and the wisdom literature, which appears throughout the ancient Near East, is filled with admonitions to scribes to avoid abusing their positions for either political or personal ends.

In Jerusalem both the royal palace and its chapel (the temple) had numerous scribes in constant employment. Most of the work would have been the day-to-day upkeep of the capital city and the wider bureaucracy of Judah, but their work also would have included keeping records of the events of the rulers' reigns and composing liturgical texts for the temple rituals. In addition, scribes throughout the ancient world liked to compose literary works that demonstrated their own knowledge and cleverness, both narratives and poems; this type of behavior appears in the Bible as well. All of the books of the Hebrew Bible came from the ranks of these educated and influential scribes.

Origins of the Torah

Clearly, the appearance of the Pentateuch in all biblical canons suggests that it was the earliest group of books to attain the status of religious authority in the biblical tradition. The "Documentary Hypothesis" posits at least four sources used to construct the first five books of the Bible. It is no longer possible to date the composition of the sources, as was supposed only a decade or two ago; but the existence of major traditions in the Torah is quite clear. One source, called the Yahwist (from the Name of God, which it uses regularly), presents engaging stories with a familiar, anthropomorphic view of God (meaning God looks and acts like a human) and a pessimistic vision of human nature. In the nineteenth century the Yahwist was dated as early as the reigns of David and Solomon (early tenth century B.C.E.), but recently scholars have argued for a date no earlier than the Babylonian exile (587–538 B.C.E.). The other primarily narrative source is the Elohist (named after the generic word for God that it prefers), written by an author who likes to separate God from humans by using prophets, angels, dreams, or visions to hold its dignified God at a distance from humanity. The Elohist originally had been dated to the time of Jeroboam's establishment of the northern Kingdom (at least in the early Kingdom of Israel, late tenth to early ninth centuries B.C.E.), but it also has recently been redated later (or even argued to have been part of the Yahwist's narrative and not an independent source altogether). The Priestly source relates genealogies, cultic material, and a God who is majestic, all-powerful, and all-knowing. Usually the Priestly source is assumed to be Post-Exilic (after 538 B.C.E.); though one school of thought argues that the priestly material came from the seventh century cultic circles of Judah. The Deuteronomist was responsible for the Book of Deuteronomy, which relates the giving of the law for a second time (hence the name: "Second Law"). Deuteronomy has been connected by Christians with King Josiah's cultic reform (±622 B.C.E.) since the fourth century C.E.; a position which is still held by the majority of Christian scholars, though others argue for an Exilic (587–538 B.C.E.), or even Post-Exilic date.

These four sources, along with other materials from the religious and cultural circles of Judah, formed the content of the Torah, which was composed early in the Second Temple Period (538 B.C.E.–70 C.E.). By tradition, Ezra, a Jewish scribe working in the Persian bureaucracy, compiled the Torah from earlier traditions while employed in Mesopotamia by the Persian government; he then took it to Palestine, where it was declared the official foundation for local Jewish religious and social government as well as ritual. That would date the formation and canonization of the Torah to roughly 400 B.C.E. Under Persian sanction it was accepted by both Jews and Samaritans as the authoritative rendition of the origins of both of their peoples and their laws.

Origins of the Prophets

The Prophets section of the Tanak is first recorded as established by 180 B.C.E. in the Book of Sirach (Ecclesiasticus). The Former Prophets, Joshua through Kings, is a series of books dealing with segments of the history of Judah and Israel. Some scholars treat these as a single work (to which they add Deuteronomy as a preface) and call it "The Deuteronomistic History" because of its recurring vocabulary and theology. Though debate rages as to whether there were earlier editions of the history (Hezekiah and Josiah are both said to have first had the history written), it is agreed by everyone that the books in their current form cannot predate the Babylonian exile (587–538 B.C.E.) for the simple reason that Second Kings ends in Babylonia with the exiled King Jehoiachin of Judah. Other scholars insist that the Former Prophets were not part of a single history, but individual works that were edited together only at the time they were recognized as sacred, to form a historical succession relating the story of the former independent states of Judah and Israel from the viewpoint of a Jerusalem incorporated into the Persian Empire. The identity of neither the authors nor the editors of these texts is known.

The books of the various prophets, with the exception of Jonah (which is a short story rather than a collection of prophetic statements) undoubtedly have their origins with the prophets bearing their names. The earliest of these is Amos, who prophesied ±750 B.C.E., and the latest is the prophet called Malachi (literally: "my messenger"; this may be an anonymous prophet, or a collection from different prophets), probably from the fifth century B.C.E. The three books referred to as the Major Prophets are all edited texts coming from the Post-Exilic Period; each includes sayings attributed to the named prophet of the title, prose accounts of aspects of the prophets' lives, editorial notations, and prophecies from others seen in the same prophetic tradition. The Book of the Twelve contains eleven (probably) previously independent collections of sayings that were themselves edited in the fourth century B.C.E., along with the prose short story of Jonah. The editor of the entire Book of the Twelve clearly manipulated some of the material in the individual books, including adding consistent editorial notations throughout. Major additonal late editing has been argued for most of the prophets in the collection. The entire collection of the Prophets must have been regarded as a sacred unit by the end of the third century B.C.E. and so a product of the Persian Period.

Origins of the Writings

The authors of the New Testament often refer to their scriptures as "the Law and the Prophets," by which they named the Torah and the Prophets as the accepted canon of their day. Both early Jewish and the earliest Christian (which were Jewish as well) communities held the Torah and the Prophets as sacred texts, but the Writings (which are occasionally also mentioned as a group in the New Testament) appear to have been determined on a congregation-by-congregation basis in the first century C.E. It has long been noticed that the Letter of Jude was written from a community that accepted both Enoch and the Assumption of Moses as authoritative scripture (the former found now only in the Ethiopian Orthodox canon and the latter in no modern canon at all, though part of the text has been recovered, including the section referred to by Jude).

As far as can be determined, every Jewish and Christian community accepted the Book of Psalms in their collection of Writings. The book contains poems related to the worship of Yahweh in Jerusalem. Many of the psalms date from the time of the First Temple (mid-tenth century to 582 B.C.E.); however, they were not collected until the Second Temple Period and appear to have played a part in Temple worship from 515 B.C.E. to 70 C.E. The meaning of specific passages in the book as it was understood by the Jewish community can be seen to have changed through this period; yet by the time early Christians read the psalms, the texts were accepted as prophecies with a canonical authority.

Some books had very complicated histories. A convenient example is the Book of Daniel, which consists of a series of short stories in chapters 1–6, a series of visions in chapters 7–12, and three more short stories in chapters 13–14 (if one's canon has the longer version of Daniel). The character of Danil (no, that is not misspelled) as a pious, wise, and loyal figure is first known from the story of Aqhat, a mythological legend found at the site of ancient Ugarit (modern Ras Shamra, on the north end of the western Mediterranean coast) from the twelth century B.C.E.; this seems to be the Danil who is mentioned by Ezekiel (14:14; note the spelling "Daniel" is that of the Book of Daniel). The stories of Nebuchadnezzar in Daniel, chapters 2–5, are clearly related to events in the reigns of both Nebuchadnezzar II and Nabonidus of the Neo-Babylonian Empire (two rulers separated by three other minor rulers: 604–562 and 555–539 B.C.E., respectively). These stories (which, by the way, appear not in Hebrew, but Aramaic) may well derive from Babylonian sources, which would explain the Akkadian names given for the supposedly Hebrew protagonists. Into these stories were added narratives of Jewish exiles as stereotyped characters, whose piety brings them through events of certain death; the Jewish rendition of these stories appears to have been composed in the Post-Exilic period and, in their current revised form, derive from the persecutions of the Jews by the Seleucid (=Greek Hellenistic ruling family) King Antiochus IV (175–163 B.C.E.) in Judea, where these (and other similar) tales served to bolster Jewish faith in the face of royal condemnation.

The visions of Daniel present an apocalyptic world where hidden events of the future are revealed to Daniel in the first days of the Persian Period (538+ B.C.E.), regarding Judean history as a progression through the persecutions of Antiochus IV down to the year 164 B.C.E. These texts derive from 164 B.C.E. since the "foretold" history is, if symbolically told, accurate enough down to the events of 164 and then no longer obtain (leaving many modern Christians to assume that the visions were really from 538 B.C.E. and the last few foretold visions are yet to occur). The Greek manuscripts show that Alexandrian Jews had an edition of the text with an added pious song for Daniel's three friends to sing in the fiery furnace as well as a trial story for Daniel and a pair of related cultic stories about faith in Yahweh as opposed to faith in Bel (=Marduk, patron deity of Babylon) or a snake; all of which were probably already additions to the Hebrew manuscript used to translate the Greek text used in Egypt, maybe around 100 B.C.E.. The authors of any of this material are quite unknown, and it is wise to remember that this reconstruction is much too simplified to demonstrate the actual production of the Book of Daniel. However, Daniel has always been a part of the Writings in Jewish tradition, being given little authority, while Christians treated the book as that of a major prophet, placing it after Ezekiel and using it for unending apocalyptic theories.

Short stories, as was just seen in Daniel, were popular throughout the Jewish religious communities. Of these, Ruth and Esther became canonical books in their own right; Judith, though very popular thoroughout Jewish history, was not accepted into the Palestinian Jewish canon, though it was in the Alexandrian and from there was taken into the Christian canon. Tobit, which appears in a longer and a shorter rendition, never had the enthusiastic audience of the other stories; nonetheless, it was in the Alexandrian canon and thereby became part of the Christian Bible. These books are anonymous literary productions, historically fictitious, but with a serious theological or social point to make. Clearly written to both entertain and to instruct, the short stories (including Jonah) all appear to have been written from the late Persian Period to the time of the Antiochan persecution, a two-hundred-year period ending ca. 160 B.C.E.

Wisdom literature forms a whole tradition by itself. In the ancient Near East, wisdom writings had been popular among scribes since the third millennium in both Mesopotamia and Egypt. Proverbs presents a classic example of the genre: the world is rational; those who are good have a good life, but those who are evil will have a bad fate. Probably a product of the Jerusalem palace staff in the days of Judah, prior to the exile, Proverbs was attributed to Solomon, as were many wisdom texts, canonical and not, but the authors are in fact unknown. A skeptical reaction to this orderly, benign worldview, can be found in the canonical books of Job and Ecclesiastes. Job presents a world where the very norms of the standard wisdom tradition create humiliation and pain for the most righteous person possible; it is a well-crafted investigation of an apparently perverse universe and a God who may be humanity's worst enemy. Ecclesiastes presents a world where everything is totally arbitrary; the actions of individuals cannot determine their fates and death is the only end that can be expected. Job and Ecclesiastes are usually dated to the aftermath of the exile and the Hellenistic Period respectively; the identity of the author of neither work is known. However, such pessimism was answered in the canon by the books of Baruch, Ecclesiasticus, and the Wisdom of Solomon; works that date from 180 B.C.E. (Ecclesiasticus) to perhaps as late as 50 C.E. (Wisdom of Solomon). These authors (and the author of Ecclesiasticus is named in the work: Jesus ben Sirach) argue that the old wisdom traditions are still true, but one must be loyal to the Torah, the cult in Jerusalem, and personal righteousness, respectively, for the system to function. In this series of books we can see a continuing intellectual debate within the scribal circles on the rationality of the world and the place of humans in God's scheme.

Lamentations is a collection of five songs composed for the commemoration of the destruction of the Temple in Jerusalem. They probably date from sometime beginning soon after the destruction of the Temple in 587 B.C.E. down to early in the Persian Period (fifth century). Because rabbinic traditions declared Jeremiah the author, Christian Bibles generally place the book immediately after Jeremiah, but the author or authors are unknown. The Song of Songs, a book filled with erotic sexuality, seems a strange volume to appear as a canonical text. Its origins appear to be in popular, secular love songs for which parallels may be found from ancient Egypt. Yet, since Rabbi Aqiba declared (in the second century C.E.) that it was the greatest book of all those in the canon, read as an allegory, it has never been doubted as sacred text. It traditionally has been treated as a composition by Solomon during his youth, though its true author or authors remain unknown, and, until the nineteenth century, was treated both in Jewish and Christian scholarship solely as an allegory about God's love for the faithful.

First and Second Chronicles, Ezra, and Nehemiah have generally been treated as a historical series in much the same way as have the Former Prophets. Though the notion that the four books (originally two scrolls: Chronicles and Ezra) were written by the same author remains popular, there are many reasons to be less than certain of their single authorship. The books are clearly products of the Persian Period (538–333 B.C.E.), though when during that period they were composed is a matter of current debate, covering the entire time span from the time of Ezra (ca. 400 B.C.E.) to the end of the empire. Usually, it is assumed that some notes deriving from Ezra and Nehemiah actually appear in the texts, but debate swirls around which passages, if any, are indeed from these men.

The four books of Maccabees are not a series. The First Book of Maccabees is a product of Hasmonaean circles (the dynasty which took over the rule of Judea after the revolt led by Mattathias against Antiochus IV, 167–163 B.C.E.) and relates the story of the sons of Mattathias in such a manner as to urge readers to obey their descendants as legitimate rulers. It was composed about 100 B.C.E. Second Maccabees relates part of the same history, but urges its readers to spurn the Hasmonaeans as unrighteous breakers of Torah. It was written about 90 B.C.E., by condensing a five-volume work written by Jason of Cyrene. Third Maccabees deals with the Jews in Alexandria, Egypt, describing some legendary escapes from destruction; written in Alexandria probably in the first half of the first century B.C.E. Fourth Maccabees, on the other hand, is a philosophical treatise on the passions that probably was composed in the first half of the first century C.E. by a Greek-cultured Jewish philosopher.

The books known as First and Second Esdras are both about Ezra and both are later than the Book of Ezra. First Esdras probably was written in the middle of the second century B.C.E. and Second Esdras in the first century C.E. First Esdras retells the story of Ezra's mission from Persia to Judea, with a historical background beginning with the cultic reform of Josiah. Second Esdras presents a series of visions ascribed to Ezra that seem to reflect the chaos of rabbinic thought on the nature of evil prior to the destruction of the Temple by the Romans in 70 C.E.

Finally, the Ethiopian Orthodox books have their own origins. Enoch is a vast work that contains a vision of heaven, a history of the Jews from the beginning to the Hellenistic Period, a history and description of the angels (heavenly and fallen), and discourses on righteousness. In its current form the book was collected in the first century C.E. though it has a truly complicated literary history containing entire earlier works and parts of numerous, now lost, Jewish literary materials within it. The Book of Jubilees retells the early history of the world through the life of Moses, adapting the earlier biblical narratives with legends and telling the story as if early biblical figures kept the later laws of Judaism. The entire work is written as if it were the presentation of God's angel to Moses on Sinai, with a foretelling of future events as well as past. It was written in Palestine ±150 B.C.E.

New Testament Origins

The early church had the Torah and the Prophets (as well as assorted other works making up different Writings in different communities) as its Bible. None of the books that now make up the New Testament were orginially written to be scripture; rather, they were written to interpret scripture. The material was composed to instruct individual congregations, which is certainly true of the Gospels, or to be sent around among congregations for educational purposes. Some of the letters were written specifically for problems in a given church but were collected and exchanged because those who received them believed that others could benefit from the content.

Those Who Wrote the Books of the New Testament

Aside from Paul, we know little about the people who wrote the New Testament books. These works were the product of literate Christians, but not professional scribes. Indeed, the majority of the "books" of the New Testament are actually letters intended for churches of the first century. Paul was the first author to have Christian material saved in the canon. Trained both in Hellenistic Greek culture and Pharasaic Judaism, Paul in his letters presumes a knowledge of both traditions on the part of his readers. Several of the canonical letters were written pseudonymously under the names of Paul and Peter. Though the letter of James may well have been written by someone named James, he appears to be neither the apostle nor Jesus' brother, the head of the church in Jerusalem.

The earliest collection of texts that became the New Testament was a compendium of Paul's letters that was circulated among the churches by 100 C.E. Paul wrote his letters to particular churches and individuals from 50 to ±58 C.E. To these letters were added others by those who knew him and wrote in his name (Colossians and Ephesians) and the Pastorals (First and Second Timothy, Titus), though the latter usually either appeared in lists of Paul's letters or not depending on whether the collector thought they were actually by Paul himself. Indeed, the first New Testament canon was compiled by Marcion (generally considered the first Christian heretic) in the middle of the second century C.E. and consisted merely of one of these lists of Paul's letters (one not containing the Pastorals) and a Gospel that looked to Christians outside of Marcion's community like an edited version of Luke.

Gospel Origins

The four Gospels were only some of the more than fifty known Gospels produced by the very early church. By late in the second century these four had clearly become the most widely accepted. Mark appears to have been the first written, perhaps as early as 70 C.E.; Matthew, Luke, and John probably appeared ±90 C.E. Only Matthew and John can be fairly certainly ascribed a place of origin: Antioch and Asia Minor (Ephesus, often assumed to be the city of John's composition, may be too specific) respectively. No one knows who wrote any of the four books; the names associated with them were ascribed to the most famous Gospels late in the second century C.E., a hundred years after their composition. All four were written in Greek and therefore deal in translations of the Aramaic or Hebrew speech that is assumed to have been the language Jesus used for teaching, as it was of other rabbis of the time. The Book of Acts of the Apostles was the second volume to the Gospel of Luke and was written only a few years after that Gospel.

While Mark, Matthew, and Luke have a number of stories in common, they tell them differently; however, Jesus consistently tells parables in these three Gospels. The first three, therefore, are called "Synoptic Gospels" (meaning they look alike) and numerous theories have been advanced about the reasons for the similarities. The most popular current notion is that Mark was used by the authors of the other two Gospels along with some written collection of Jesus' sayings (called by scholars "Q" from the German "Quelle" = "source"). John, on the other hand, was the product of a different early Christian tradition, presenting Jesus as someone who engaged in dialogues with people who barely understood him. The Passion narrative in all four Gospels follows the same outline, however, so it may well have been the first part of the story of Jesus that became standardized in the early church.

The Other New Testament Authors

The catholic epistles were written to be circulated among a number of churches and were written during roughly 90–120 C.E., though Second Peter has been dated as late as the middle of the second century by some scholars. These letters were written in the names of persons of some importance in the churches of that time by anonymous authors who felt they had to use their teachers' names, a form of letter writing common enough in the first century C.E. by disciples, real or supposed, of great philosophers. Usually the church associated the letters with the names of persons who actually appeared in the Gospels or Acts when it came time to consider them for the canon. The extent to which any of them may be related to the apostles themselves remains debated. The letters of Clement fit into this same pattern, including the date of their composition and questions of authorship.

The Revelation to John was written in Asia Minor ±95 C.E. and describes the Roman Empire as seen through the eyes of the Johannine Christian community (the community that produced the Gospel of John) as the first major persecution crept over the Empire. Though the persecution of Domitian did not actually affect the church in Asia Minor itself, the author (unknown, but writing in the name of the apostle John) saw the empire as demonic and attacking the church on behalf of Satan and the forces of evil. Revelation presents the visions that explain what the events on earth really meant for the universe.

The Coptic use of the Apostolic Constitutions is unique in canonical tradition. The "Constitutions" are eight books of church legislation from Syria, collected in the fourth century. By tradition, the collection is derived from Bishop Clement of Rome, but the actual origins of these texts have been lost to history.

Questions for Reflection and Discussion

1. What difference does it make whether the Bible was written all at once or over a long period of time?

2. If you have a Bible with more than one rendition of the same history, how does the community or tradition deal with contradictions in the material [First and Second Maccabees, for example, have opposed views on the central characters]?

3. What does the addition of the New Testament books to the Torah and Prophets do for Christian interpretation of the books they share with the Jewish community?

4. Could there have been more books in your canon; could they be written now?

5. How does a work written by a human, for a particular purpose, become understood as the very word of God? Or, taking the other tack, how does the very word of God become understood as human words?

Bibiliographical Note

The origin of the biblical books are commonly covered in introductions to the Bible. For those Old Testament books not in the Hebrew Bible, James H. Charlesworth, ed., *The Old Testament Pseudepigrapha*, 2 vols. (Garden City, N.Y.: Doubleday, 1983, 1985), and Jacob M. Myers, *I & II Esdras*, Anchor Bible (Garden City,N.Y. Doubleday, 1974), were used for background. For the world of the scribe in the ancient Near East see: John G. Gammie and Leo G. Perdue, eds., *The Sage in Israel and the Ancient Near East* (Winona Lake, Ind.: Eisenbrauns, 1990). Several volumes deal with the formation of the canon; among those easy to read for the beginner are: John W. Miller, *The Origins of the Bible: Rethinking Canon History* (New York: Paulist, 1994); Lee Martin McDonald, *The Formation of the Christian Biblical Canon* (Nashville: Abingdon Press, 1988); James A. Sanders, *From Sacred Story to Sacred Text* (Philadelphia: Fortress, 1987). Harry Y. Gamble, *The New Testament Canon: Its Making and Meaning* (Philadelphia: Fortress, 1985), presents a short introduction to the rise of the New Testament books.

What It Really Says: The Text Of The Bible

We have no original manuscripts of any of the books of the Bible. When we pick up a copy of the Bible to read, it is usually in a modern translation that we assume bears the meaning of the words of some Hebrew, Aramaic, or Greek text. Debate in scholarly circles often surrounds the modern translations, but there is just as much debate surrounding the actual text of the Hebrew, Aramaic, or Greek texts from which the translations are made.

The attempt to create a biblical text in the original languages is known as "Textual Criticism" and is common throughout the biblical scholarship of Western Christianity. For reasons that may become clearer in the following, many Orthodox Christians and most Jewish scholars are not as engaged in textual studies.

Textual Criticism and Its Goals

Current Bible translations are dependent on the work of previous generations in reconstructing the early forms of the books of the Bible. There are essentially two different goals for these studies.

One group of scholars attempts to reconstruct the original text of a given book as it was first written down by its first author. Textual criticism had its beginning in this search for the first formulation. It is understood by those engaged in this type of research that the first text would be the most authoritative. Many textual scholars would argue that the author's manuscript would be the word of God itself; others only that the original would have the clearest presentation of the author's intent. In either case, numerous manuscript variations are compared in an attempt to determine which of the variations is most likely to have been the original from which the others deviated. Occasionally, several variants are used to produce a hypothetical original text for which there are no manuscripts that bear that reading. Few scholars in this endeavor believe we have as yet recovered the original text of any book of the Bible.

The other goal sought by textual scholars is to create the best possible manuscript of any given biblical book. Given that there are no original manuscripts from the hand of the first author for any book in the canon (and there is no hope of finding any such manuscript), the best that can be achieved is to reconstruct from various existing manuscripts the most reasonable text of each book. There is also the recognition among many of those engaged in this type of research that the original author's manuscript was not a biblical text. That is to say, one is only dealing with the text of the Bible at the point at which a given book has been declared to be part of a canon. By that time a book may have been edited several times. For example, there was no Book of Amos in any canon prior to its having been edited into the Book of the Twelve, since it was the Book of the Twelve that was declared canonical, and only later was Amos divided out of the larger scroll to stand as a book on its own, by which time it contained the editorial notations now understood to be part of the Book of Amos. Scholars of this tradition would be interested in the earlier material edited for the Book of the Twelve, but primarily are interested in recreating the best possible text for the Book of Amos as biblical text.

What We Translate

Should one head for seminary, the texts one is most apt to be confronted with as the Bible in its original languages are:

> *Biblia Hebraica Stuttgartensia,* edited by R. Kittel and others (Stuttgart: Deutsche Bibelgesellschaft, 1983). This is the Hebrew and Aramaic Tanak with pointing (vowels) and division markers, accents, and notes based on the Leningrad Codex, which is the oldest complete Hebrew

Bible (ca. 1000 C.E.). This work reproduces that manuscript, complete with copying errors, but provides students with a copy of the earliest full text of the Hebrew Bible.

Septuaginta, edited by Alfred Rahlfs (Stuttgart: Deutsche Bibelgesellschaft, 1935). This is the standard introductory edition of the edited text of the Septuagint (the Greek Bible used by the Jews of ancient Alexandria, Egypt). It is a Greek text compiled from several Septuagint manuscripts. In general usage, the books that were collected by Rahlfs have come to be known as the books of the Septuagint, but the manuscript traditions contained works not included in this addition.

The Greek New Testament, edited by Kurt Aland and others (assorted Bible Societies, including the ABS, continuing updates). An ever-reedited Greek text of the New Testament books with numerous variant readings in the footnotes. Literally thousands of manuscripts are consulted to reconstruct the texts that appear herein, and editorial debates change readings on a fairly steady basis.(It should be noted that New Testament scholars tend to use a different Greek text, known generally as "Nestle-Aland.")

There are several other editions of biblical language texts available, and some religious traditions prefer other editions; however, all texts that are used for Bible translating in the Western Christian churches are edited texts.

When modern translators set out to make a new translation of the Bible, they have to begin by determining which Hebrew, Aramaic, or Greek text they are intending to translate. Few modern translations are based on a single manuscript; instead they depend on textual critical reconstructions from several ancient manuscripts. However, the above-mentioned texts remain standard references for the endeavor (although Rahlfs is being replaced currently by a series of new volumes called "The Göttingen Septuagint"; textual studies never stand still).

Hebrew Bible

The Tanak has a textual tradition that extends back to the eighth century C.E. Prior to the standardization of the canonical texts by the Masoretes (a group dedicated to the preservation of the exact canonical forms of the books of the Bible and to a literal reading of those texts) there was no set form to any of the books in the canon. Since the formation of the Masoretic Text, Jewish scrolls and bound Bibles have followed its formal text of the Hebrew and Aramaic. Until printing presses entered the western world, all copies of the Tanak were copied by hand, so there are still several variations among the many manuscripts; however, it is possible to determine the accepted Masoretic textual form because there are numerous manuscripts, and the Masoretes counted the words in every book and recorded the count at the end of each book when copied. Unfortunately, the Masoretes did not quite agree among themselves as to the exact text, so there are a couple of Masoretic traditions that provide a very few differences in their own manuscripts.

Since one form of the Masoretic Text has become the official Bible in the Jewish tradition, Jewish Bible translations into modern languages are based on one text, the official Masoretic. However, Christian scholars dealing with the Hebrew books of their Bible begin with the Masoretic Text, but supplement their translations with earlier Hebrew manuscripts. The most extensive early Hebrew texts are those that were found at the northwest edge of the Dead Sea hidden away in pottery jars during the first century C.E.

Almost any introduction to the Hebrew Bible contains a mention (if not a picture) of the Great Isaiah Scroll from the Dead Sea caves. It is usually mentioned as having the same Hebrew text as the Masoretic Text of the Leningrad Codex, as well as being the oldest complete Hebrew manuscript of a biblical book. It is close to being a complete text, but small sections along the bottom of the length of the scroll are missing and, while the text is very similar to the Masoretic Text, the spelling of words is quite different and there are a series of minor word changes (many of which are clearly scribal copying errors). What the introductions to the Hebrew Bible usually do not mention is that there are other Isaiah scrolls less similar to the Masoretic Text. Which suggests that if these all came from one community (which is not at all certain), they had more than one version of the Book of Isaiah, each being used as a sacred book, but that the textual content of the book itself was not yet considered sacred enough to be standardized.

In fact, portions of all the canonical texts of the Hebrew Bible except Esther are attested among the scrolls, as well as fragments and citations of many of the books that appear in the Christian Old Testaments beyond the canon of the Tanak. However, the Jeremiah scroll does not conform to the later Masoretic Text, but is a Hebrew text along the line of the book of Jeremiah found in the Septuagint tradition (a differently written content ordered in a different fashion from the Masoretic Text). This demonstrates that the Septuagint Greek text was not a sloppily made copy of our Hebrew Jeremiah, but a decent copy of a different Hebrew text than that which became accepted in Palestine. The Samaritan Pentateuch also makes an appearance among the bits and pieces of Dead Sea Scrolls; so two versions of the Torah show up in the caves. It is clear from these fragments that, though books were declared canonical, in the first century C.E. the texts of the canonical books appeared in several forms. That being the case, it poses a problem for the textual critic who wishes to determine which of these variations represents the earlier, or more accurate, textual tradition.

But there are more manuscripts to choose from. Everything from medieval Cairo synagogue scrolls (which were set in a special room when they were wearing out and so were preserved because of the closed room; anything with the divine name written upon it is considered too sacred to be destroyed in Orthodox Jewish tradition, so synagogues from early times have a *genizah* for scrolls that have become too worn to be used anymore) to bits of mummy encasing strips taken from Deuteronomy used by ancient Egyptian undertakers (the book of Deuteronomy was merely scrap paper to the Egyptians) provide portions of Hebrew biblical texts. Many of these have variations in spelling and wording. Yet modern translators, almost without exception, accept the Masoretic Text as the base on which to adapt other textual attestations.

Greek Bibles: Old Testament

The Septuagint series of manuscripts contains different collections of books. All contain a certain core of books, covering essentially the Greek translations of the Hebrew Bible and certain Deuterocanonical books. The Septuagint was the product of the Alexandrian Jewish community, which wanted a copy of the biblical books in its everyday language, since Greek was necessary for daily life (Alexandria was a Greek city in Egypt, founded by Alexander the Great— and named after him).

There are numerous copies of the Greek Old Testament Bible. A number of additions and some subtractions from the text of the Hebrew Bible as we know it occur regularly in the various manuscripts; many of these clearly were written into the Hebrew text before the time of the translators as amplifications to the Hebrew narratives (the retelling of Esther is the most glaring example of this) and some appear to have come from other Hebrew textual traditions than that behind the Masoretic Text (both the Samaritan Pentateuch and the Septuagint add to Cain's comment to Abel in Genesis 4:8 a phrase that appears to make the murder premeditated). And, of course, the Deuterocanonicals appear in the Septuagint manuscripts but not in the Palestinian Hebrew canons.

As with the Hebrew manuscripts, the Greek Bibles were hand copies that produced a number of variants in the text. Since there was a tradition that the books being copied already had the status of sacred text, the number of differences among the Septuagint texts in manuscript is smaller than one might suspect. However, the differences between the Hebrew being translated and the Greek into which the works were being translated often proved to be major, the classic example being the changing of the Hebrew "young woman" of Isaiah 7:14, to the Greek "virgin" (enough said).

Because the Greek manuscripts formed the basis of Christian Bibles, the early Christian Old Testaments conformed to the books as they were produced in Alexandrian Greek. The Greek Esther and the Greek Daniel are obvious examples of books with additions to the Hebrew texts. Some books simply had two versions; Tobit has a longer text (English translations in the New English Bible and the New American Bible) and a shorter text (as in the Revised Standard Version) both of which appear in Bibles and both of which are "canonical." Yet other books, like Job, had a change in tone through the process of translation, such that the church picked up the Greek twist on the narrative (the heavenly officer of the Hebrew text, "The Divine Prosecutor" has become Satan, "the devil," a rather major change that would color all further use of the Book of Job in all Christian traditions). When the official Catholic Latin Bible (the Vulgate, translated mostly by Jerome) was in production, consultation was made with contemporary rabbis, and changes were made in the Septuagint text being translated to conform to the Hebrew Text where Jerome's theology would allow such changes. This produced a rather critical edition for its time of a Greek text as the basis of the Latin Bible's Old Testament. Much of the Septuagint textual tradition passed into Western Christian Bibles through use of the standardized Latin Vulgate.

Greek Bibles: New Testament

The Old Testament textual critical work seems too simple for words when set against the problems of determining a text for the New Testament books. The early church did not consider these books sacred and so were not terribly careful about copying them. If someone wanted a copy of the Gospel of Mark, but wanted a resurrection narrative at the end of it, they added it. If another wanted the Gospel of Luke, but preferred Matthew's telling of a particular story, they put Matthew's version in Luke's Gospel where they wanted it. If someone didn't like what Paul said about some particular thing, they left it out, or added something extra to make up for it. They corrected the Greek vocabulary, they corrected the grammar, they corrected the stories, the letters, the symbolism. In short, from the over 5,000 Greek manuscripts of early New Testament books (and then there are the early translations into Latin, Syriac, Aramaic, Gothic, Coptic, and so forth) there are a staggering two hundred thousand variant readings.

There is no Masoretic textual tradition for New Testament books. By the time the Bishops at the North African Council in Carthage in 397 C.E. determined the canon for the New Testament they were discussing books for which each of them, in their home parishes, was using a slightly different text. Many of the differences are minor, but almost every chapter of every book in the New Testament has phrases that appear in some manuscripts and not in others. Sometimes it can be easily determined that a given manuscript was written by someone paraphrasing a text, or changing texts to their liking, but more often the problem is to discern among several equally possible readings as to which is better or earlier.

The earliest New Testament manuscripts are from Egypt and are bits and pieces of books made from papyrus (water reeds whose stalks were split and then glued together crosswise to make sheets). Most of these are small parts of a text, though a nearly complete copy of a book of Paul's letters from ±300 C.E. has survived with enough strange changes to interest almost anyone (the compiler believed Hebrews to be a letter of Paul but did not believe the Pastorals were Pauline, while Romans 16 is treated as a separate letter by Paul altogether).

The manuscripts that are the most important for early New Testament textual criticism are known as "uncials." These are texts written entirely in capital Greek letters and on parchment (scraped animal hide). These were codices and often contained both the Old and New Testaments. The two most important of the ±250 known uncials are referred to as Codex Sinaiticus (because it was discovered by Western scholars at Saint Catherine's Monastery at Mount Sinai—the monks already knew about it) and Codex Vaticanus (because it is part of the Vatican library collection). Both codices were copied in the fourth century, and both contain more books than the New Testament now contains; however, they provide early and nearly complete texts of the New Testament books, though, of course, with differences. Indeed, the parchment codices have traditionally been divided into "Western" and "Eastern" traditions, with some manuscripts using aspects of both traditions. Major differences can be followed through the two trajectories, but the individual manuscripts in both traditions had plenty of unique readings of their own. Thus, the texts of the canonical New Testament books were not as established as even the texts of the Old Testament books in use at the same time.

The Byzantium Church used its own Greek manuscript; based on an uncertain textual tradition of the early church, it was used for public readings of the Bible throughout the existence of the Byzantine Empire and so has become accepted as authoritative in the Greek Orthodox Church. Generally simply called the Byzantine text, its origins, both for the Old and New Testaments, appear to have been texts in use before the reign of Constantine. Other Greek manuscripts are considered by many in the Orthodox churches as inferior and are generally dismissed by Orthodox scholars in favor of the established text. Having an established text in the Orthodox tradition precludes the need for extensive textual studies as done in the Western churches, where the official Bible had been a Latin translation, insofar as there was an established text at all.

In 1515 Erasmus of Rotterdam began work on an edited Greek New Testament, using such early Greek manuscripts as were available to him at the time (neither Sinaiticus nor Vaticanus was yet known in scholarly circles); the finished product was published in 1516 and became the basis for all New Testament translations throughout Europe and the Americas until the late nineteenth century. All the canonical books of the New Testament were studied and provided with a critical Greek text. The only problem was the very end of the Book of Revelation, for which there were no extant Greek manuscripts; Erasmus solved this problem by translating the Vulgate Latin into Greek. Other scholars added to Erasmus' Greek text notes and comparisons with another early Greek manuscript and in 1624 an advertising campaign by Elzevir Publishers in the Netherlands proclaimed that you too could buy the accepted "received text" of the Greek Bible. The advertising pitch phrase "Textus Receptus" caught on and is used to this day for the Erasmus Greek Bible. Many, particularly conservative, Christian denominations continue to use Erasmus' Greek text as the definitive Greek New Testament text and so do no other textual studies.

A Little Overlap

When the New Testament authors quoted their Bible they quoted what they were familiar with in their own religious life. Since the writers of the New Testament texts wrote Greek, they quoted the Greek Bible. For modern translators this presents a problem. As shown above, the Greek Septuagint text was not the same as that of the Hebrew Tanak. Moreover, there were other Greek translations of the Bible in use at that time that were outside the circles of the Septuagint manuscripts, so the New Testament has quotations of the "Law and the Prophets," some of which are found in the Septuagint, some of which are from other Greek translations, and some of which have no extant parallels.

Of course, occasionally the New Testament citation will be to the Hebrew text. The cry of Jesus on the cross in Mark 15:34 makes sense in context only if the quote is kept in the Hebrew, since the passage is describing the misunderstanding of the people around the cross, hearing "Eloi" as "Eliya." Moreover, Jesus quoting the first line of the psalm conforms to rabbinic traditions of citing an entire psalm by quoting its first line.

For the modern translator who wishes to use the best early Hebrew text for the Old Testament and the best early Greek New Testament text in a Bible containing both testaments, this produces a problem. Most of the quotations in the New Testament made from the Old Testament will not be the same in English when the translator finishes translating from the best manuscripts, since the Greek New Testament represents the Greek Old Testament tradition and the Hebrew Old Testament represents another tradition. The usual manners of dealing with this problem have been to translate the Greek as it appears and let the reader wonder about the difference, to change the Greek a bit to make it conform more to the Hebrew translation in the Old Testament, or to place a footnote in at the bottom of the text explaining the difference.

Questions for Reflection and Discussion

1. What is the difference between having a canonical book and having an established textual content for that book?

2. Is there then a difference between the Bibles of the church's Old Testament (Greek tradition) and the Tanak (Hebrew tradition), or can one just switch them around? Contemplate the Protestant Bible, which uses the Greek New Testament , and the Hebrew Bible for its Old Testament.

3. What problems can you imagine related to having to create the basic text before you can translate it?

4. Some Jewish and Christian traditions hold that the text has been kept pure as God dictated it; how can that position be adapted to the textual traditions, or can it?

5. What happens should another early manuscript appear with yet more variations in the texts of the books it bears?

Bibliographical Note

For the Old Testament section, Ellis R. Brotzman, Old Testament *Textual Criticism: A Practical Introduction* (Grand Rapids: Baker Book House, 1994), was useful; and for the New Testament section, Helmut Koester, *Introduction to the New Testament, Volume Two: History and Literature of the Early Christianity* (Philadelphia: Fortress. Berlin: Walter de Gruyter, 1982), was helpful.

ALL THESE NUMBERS

Modern Western Bibles, and those derived from them, all have numbers scattered throughout the text. Sometimes these numbers appear in the passages themselves and sometimes down the margins of the page. These are chapter and verse markers. They are not a part of the biblical text! The purpose of the numbers is to aid readers in being able to find specific passages swiftly. They derive from early markings in manuscripts to mark off sentences, litugical readings, or scholarly notations.

What Are the Numbers?

There are always some people in Bible classes who do not understand the basic use of the numbering system. If one asks if there is anyone present who does not understand it there is always silence, but students will sit there either certain that they do know when they do not, or they have no idea but assume everyone else does and will laugh at them should they signify that they do not understand. Hence, it is best to just explain the numbers and not embarrass anyone.

If you happen to be reading a book on the Bible and you should run across the citation "Gen. 2:4b," you are being told that the author is speaking about the beginning of the Second Creation Story in Genesis. (If you don't understand the two creation narratives, check with one of the introductions mentioned in the preface materials or chapter 9 below.) Taking the citation one part at a time we find the following.

"Gen." is the standard abbreviation for the the Book of Genesis. Most books of the Bible in any Western language have a standard abbreviation, though different printers may use variations (Exodus often occurs as either Ex. or Exod.). One simply has to become familiar with the various books of the Bible and then be able to associate them with the abbreviations that appear. If one comes from a Protestant background and is reading a Catholic book, one may find abbreviations for books unknown to the reader. Most are fairly obvious: "Macc." usually appears for Maccabees, "Bar." for Baruch, "Tob." for Tobit, and so forth. However, some can surprise you: Ecclesiasticus is usually shortened to "Sirach" from the Jewish designation of the book, "The Wisdom of Jesus ben Sirach." And occasionally the Latin book names still appear in their shortened forms: "Os." is Hosea (Osee), "Soph." is Zephaniah (Sophonias), "Par." is Chronicles (Paralipomenon), and so forth. On the other hand, Catholics may see "1 Kgs." in a Protestant volume and be unaware that the author did not mean First Samuel, which in traditional Catholic Bibles was called First Kings (the first of four Books of Kings).

The first number in a biblical citation is the "chapter" number. Most books of the Bible are divided into several chapters, which tend to be marked with darkened, bold, or enlarged letters in the text or margin. Some books are too short to have such divisions, such as Obadiah in the Tanak or Jude in the New Testament. From the example, "2" preceding the colon, means that the passage appears in the second major division of the book of Genesis. Many modern Bibles place the chapter numbers at the top of the page for easy reference, so finding chapter 2 in any book means only finding the correct book and maybe turning a page.

The number after the colon is the "verse" number. Verses are the divisions within chapters. They usually correspond to sentences or long clauses in prose texts and poetic verses in poetry; however, there is no necessary correlation between the numbering system and the grammatical divisions of the text, so they cannot be used to determine anything about the actual text itself. The verses can be any length from a couple of words to several sentences (particularly in some of the Eastern Orthodox books not found in the Western churches' Bibles). So the "4" of the example says that the passage in question is the fourth section marked off in the second chapter of Genesis.

There is in the example a "b" after the verse number. Modern biblical scholars, from the nineteenth century onward, have divided some verses into smaller sections in order to designate specific parts of a verse. The "b" in this verse is almost universally understood by scholars of the Tanak, since it divides verse four into the final line of the Priestly Creation Story and the first clause of the Yawhistic Creation Story. Poetry, as in the Psalms, often has been divided into numerous subdivisions by this small letter system. Individual lines of the poetic verse or even individual cola of the lines of poetry may be given their own subdivision lower-case letter. The problem with this system at the present time is that, with a few exceptions (like the current example), different scholars may divide the same verse with different subdivisions so it is not always clear exactly which part of the verse is meant (though at least "a" always means the first part of the verse).

The colon is used in most American publications to divide the chapter number from the verse number. Other countries use other conventions, which may be confusing until you get used to them, since periods and commas are commonly used to divide these numbers. Other punctuation may denote other relationships among the numbers in a citation; a semicolon usually denotes a break between independent citations, commas break up independent verses, and hyphens or dashes denote that the passage runs from one citation to the next inclusively. Try not to confuse the following:

2:4–6:7	=	chapter 2 verse 4, through chapter 6 verse 7
2–4; 6–7	=	chapter 2 through chapter 4, and chapter 6 through chapter 7
2; 4–6:7	=	chapter 2 and chapter 4 through chapter 6 verse 7
2:4, 6–7	=	chapter 2 verse 4 and verse 6 through verse 7 (skip verse 5)
2:4; 6–7	=	chapter 2 verse 4 and chapter 6 through chapter 7

Background to the Divisions
The earliest manuscripts of the biblical books do not necessarily have any division markings on them. Certainly when Paul wrote a letter to a church he did not divide it into chapters or verses; neither did any of the other authors of canonical books. The texts

were written to be read straight through and were neither intended nor expected to need reference notations. The first divisions came about for liturgical purposes; the detailed numbering system came from scholarly debate and discussions.

The earliest divisions made in Hebrew manuscripts were simply writing stylistic devices that were not standardized. These included starting each new sentence on its own line or ending significant sections of narrative by elongating the last letter of the last sentence to fill out the scroll column. Such techniques made it easier to read the text line by line, but were not intended to aid anyone in finding anything except significant stops during reading.

The first division marks made intentionally to standardize the reading of the text (and these appear to be found already in some of the Dead Sea Scrolls) were to mark out readings for the liturgical year. It was the custom to read through the Torah in cycles of either three years (Palestinian and Egyptian lectionary) or one year (Babylonian lectionary) in the course of synagogue services. To this end small marks were made above, below, or between the words that ended and began the weekly readings, in order to assure the congregation of completing the Torah on time.

The Masoretes standardized the marking systems by using a small hanging *pe* [p] to stand for "parashah," the extent of the longer readings, and a small hanging *samek* [s] for "sidrah," the marker for shorter readings. The exact divisions were not standardized until the Masoretes (eighth century C.E.), since the purpose of the divisions was only to insure that the reading of the Torah would be covered in the course of the allotted period, not to ensure that everyone was reading the same sections of the Torah at the same time. Rabbis discussing passages of the Torah by correspondence, which has been common since before the rise of Christianity, would make use of the reading divisions to make clear what passage they were concerned about in the ensuing letter. It might be noted that these weekly readings continue in the modern synagogue where they are called the "sederim"; however, the scrolls actually read in the service are without the division markers, since the reader of the passage of the day is expected to know where to begin and where to end the Torah reading for the particular Sabbath.

Early Christian Bible manuscripts did not divide the texts. However, some Septuagint Jewish lectionary markings were adapted by Christian scribes late in the Roman Period to devise a system of chapter divisions, which were marked by the use of small symbols in the margins. These divisions were copied into the Vulgate (Latin) translation of the Bible used in Western Europe throughout the Medieval Period. It was discovered that discussions of texts over long distances could be facilitated by making reference to the chapter divisions in the same manner that rabbis could refer to their weekly Torah reading divisions. So in the Medieval Period Christians divided up their Bible manuscripts into sections. At first they used a system of symbols in the margins, then enlarged the first letter of the first word in such a section, and finally illuminated the large letters with brightly colored illustrations.

Various scholars began to number the sections, using their own notions of where the divisions should occur, but the system that became the standard for western Christendom was developed by the Archbishop of Canterbury, Stephen Langton, before his elevation to the bishopric, while he was teaching at the University of Paris early in the thirteenth century. His system was adopted for use with the official editions of the Vulgate Bible and within a century was in use thoughout Europe as a standard system to refer to passages anywhere in the Bible.

With the spirited (and often mean-spirited) polemics of biblical scholarship between Christian and Jewish scholars in the fourteenth century, it was decided by Rabbi Solomon ben Ishmael, ca. 1330, that the participants needed a common numbering system for their references. To this end he adopted the current Vulgate numbering system by finding the corresponding divisions in the Hebrew Bible (remember that the two Bibles are not exactly the same). The Hebrew numbers vary slightly in their positions in certain places from the Vulgate, often making citations from modern Hebrew texts a verse or two different from the modern Christian citations. When printing was introduced in the Western world, both Jewish and Christian publishers included the divisions developed by Stephen Langton and Solomon ben Ishmael in the printed editions of their Bibles, and thus their division system provided the numbers in use to this day.

When Numbers and Textual Criticism Collide

Since the manuscript traditions for the Bible are not the same everywhere and the numbering system that was accepted in the fourteenth century was based on a particular Vulgate text, the numbers of the Bible do not always fall in the same places when transferred to other Bibles. Moreover, with textual critical reconstructions of the

Greek New Testament often removing lines from the later Gospel narratives, in comparison with earlier Greek manuscripts, these numbers simply fall out of the text. It would produce enormous problems to renumber the ever-changing Greek texts every time something was removed or added to the accepted numbering scheme. The standard manner of dealing with such problems is simply to retain the numbers currently in use and let the text have some odd numbering sequences. A few examples of the problems follow:

Missing Verses: Textual (Matthew 23:14)

Since modern English translations of the Bible are based on critical reconstructions of the original texts, changes in the content of the Hebrew or Greek produce biblical passages different from that used by Langton. If you open your Bible to Matthew 23:14, you may or may not have a verse there. For those New Testaments based on the "Textus Receptus" there will be a "woe" saying of Jesus concerning widows' houses because the line appeared in the Latin text used by Langton to number the verses. However, most ancient manuscripts of Matthew do not have this particular verse, and those manuscripts that scholars consider to be the most reliable for the early tradition of the Gospel overwhelmingly lack it. Therefore, in the reconstruction of the Greek of the New Testament, this passage has been left out as a later addition to the original Gospel. Some modern translations, while leaving the verse out, will place a footnote where it would have appeared and print the line at the bottom of the page, noting that it appears in some Greek manuscripts. Numerous such notes appear throughout modern Bibles, though usually they are only parts of verses; for while it is common for words or phrases to have been added to or subtracted from existing sentences while scribes were copying early texts, it was less common to add or subtract entire sentences.

A Floating Story (John 7:53—8:11)

The most interesting section of numbered material is John 7:53—8:11. This is the story of the woman taken in adultery. The story appeared in Langton's Bible and was numbered in sequence. Through study of both the modern collections of manuscripts and the style of Greek in the passage, however, it is now known that the story is not really a part of the original Gospel of John. The first major clue was that some manuscripts did not contain the passage at all and others placed it earlier in the Gospel (after 7:36) or at the end as an appendix (after 21:25), while a few manuscripts had the story, but had it as part of the Gospel of Luke (after 21:38). Modern translations of John tend either to retain the narrative at the place where it is numbered by tradition or to drop the entire passage into a lengthy footnote. If the passage is printed in sequence, it may be set apart by brackets or marked with a footnote as to its dubious existence there. Again, those translations from the "Textus Receptus" will have the section but may make no note of the passage's floating nature at all.

The Strange Numbers of the Book of Psalms

The numbering system in the Book of Psalms presents its own problems. Unlike other books of the Bible, the individual psalms were given numbers early in the manuscript traditions. The usual Western number of 150 psalms in the book are not actually numbered the same in all Bibles. The confusion comes because in two cases two distinct psalms in the Hebrew manuscripts were joined together in the Septuagint to form one psalm each (Psalms 9 and 10, and 114 and 115). The total number of 150 for the series of psalms in the book is retained because Psalms 116 and 147 were both divided into two psalms each in the Septuagint. However, this means that the psalms from 9 through 146 are not numbered the same in Bibles dependent on the Septuagint (so the Vulgate and all Catholic Bibles until the twentieth century) as they are in the Hebrew Bible and the Protestant Bible dependent on it. In addition, some of the verse numbering systems shift by one or two verses in the individual psalms, so when looking up a reference from a book it might be necessary to check the verses immediately above or below the verse number as it appears in a particular Bible, as well as checking the psalm one or two poems away from the citation number, should the first passage you check make no sense relative to the book's comments.

Missing Verses: Theological (Job 42:4)

Occasionally one comes across a missing verse number that has nothing to do with the manuscript traditions but is related to scholarly theory or theological positions. The clearest case of this in a current Bible is Job 42:4. In *The New American Bible* the verse is simply missing, and the excluded text is not supplied in the footnote that appears there to explain that the verse is an interruption in the text. There are no manuscript traditions either in Hebrew or Greek that actually lack the verse; however, a number of modern scholars have noted the similarity of the phrase to one that God uses to open the speech from the storm (38:3b). Believing that Job has to be repenting of his position of innocence before God, some scholars argue that the verse was miscopied from the speech of God and therefore does not belong in the mouth of Job.

Several traditions have come together to produce this textual reconstruction, the first being, of course, that the Western church has traditionally read Job through the theology of the Septuagint, where there is a prologue pitting Good (God) and Evil (the devil) against each other. The Hebrew text has a much more ambiguous vision of the affair. Moreover, Christian reading of the text has always (until the late nineteenth century investigations of the Hebrew text) argued that the disasters befalling Job were solely the work of Satan. The Catholic Church has a long tradition of interpreting biblical texts from the Vulgate, which was the official Catholic Bible until the Second Vatican Council (1962–1965). The Vulgate, remember, came primarily from the Septuagint, and the Book of Job was understood through the Greek text when translated into Latin. The translators of the *New American Bible* wished to produce an Old Testament text from the Hebrew of the Masoretic Textual tradition, while still maintaining a Catholic Bible tradition of interpretation.

What results is an English translation of Hebrew where the theological thrust of the Greek tradition has taken precedence over the actual Hebrew text. The influence of the Greek in Christian Bibles for the Book of Job is almost universal in the opening chapters where "hasatan" in the Hebrew appears almost always as "Satan" in modern English Christian Bibles (though note that *Tanakh— The Holy Scriptures,* from the Jewish Publication Society, translates "the Adversary" with the Hebrew text). The Hebrew term is an official title meaning something like "the accuser" and is treated in these introductory passages as the divine prosecuting attorney; the Hebrew text does not present the character as anything but a heavenly functionary working for God. The Greek text has "ho diabolos," which means "the slanderer" (from which: the devil). The theological shift made with the Greek translation in the opening of the book led to the position that God is guiltless and Satan did all the evil in the book. Because of this understanding it was necessary for Job to admit he was guilty of accusing God of evil when it was really Satan who was at fault. The problem is that the Vulgate text reads with the meaning of the Septuagint slant on the story, but the Hebrew text, in fact, has God being the guilty party, and therefore Job would be wrong to repent of accusing God of the evil. The verse 42:4 belongs in the Hebrew text and needs to be translated because Job's last demand that God admit God's guilt is the finish to the Hebrew dialogue section (and it is why the prose ending is as it is). What this does for one's theology, having a biblical text that flatly states that God can be evil, is not our problem here, just that the text can be manipulated to fit the theology of the people who translate it, and one may find a missing verse number for no reason related to any textual manuscript.

Different Verses, Same Numbers? (Ending of Mark)

If several Bibles are consulted for the same chapter and verse of a book, different passages might arise. Though usually that event would occur when Jewish and Christian Bibles are consulted because of the slightly different numbering systems, one can find different passages in books with more than one canonical form. Both Esther and Tobit have two forms that appear in Bibles, and numbers from one tradition will not match the other rendition of the book. Also, Daniel 13:60 may be looked up in Catholic Bibles with the expectation of finding the shout of joy at the end of the trial, but there is no such chapter in Protestant Bibles.

One of the more unusual numbering problems, however, is the ending of Mark. It is now generally agreed among New Testament scholars that Mark ended with 16:8, wherein the women flee in fear from the empty tomb and tell no one what they have seen. However, as scribes copied the manuscript in the early church for use in their own congregations, some added resurrection passages to have the work conform to other gospels or for the benefit of their readers. The Bible that was numbered by Langton had such an addition; the one now called "the longer ending," which adds twelve more verses to the gospel. There is also a "shorter ending" which adds two sentences to 16:8, but which do not have numbers so, when published at the end of the gospel, they form a long 16:8. There is also an ending called "the Freer Logion" (from the manuscript collection where it was first discovered) which has two verses just like the longer ending and then has a three-sentence unique ending of its own; this text is so rare that no modern Bibles assume it was the original ending, but sometimes, when printed, verses 13 and 14 are given the numbers of the longer ending. However, modern Bibles can and do end with Mark 16:8, or with the longer ending, or with the shorter ending. Some modern editions of the Bible will print all three additions to the Gospel of Mark one after the other, and others will choose one of the four options and may or may not explain that there are other endings. So, what one finds when looking up Mark 16:8 or 16:9 can only be determined by the Bible one reads.

Questions for Reflection and Discussion

1. Is there any reason to be upset that the chapter and verse numbers do not always match?

2. Although the symbol and number markers were not originally used for grammatical divisions of the text, many people now use them much like periods; why would this be a problem for reading the Bible?

3. Should Bibles provide texts in footnotes of those passages the translators have deemed to be additions to the original text and so removed from their translation?

4. Since the numbering system was created in the Middle Ages and Jewish and Christian systems are different, should new consistent numbers be developed?

5. With several different Bible translations, try picking some chapter and verse numbers at random and finding what each Bible has there (even the different translations would be interesting) and it would help make certain everyone knows how to use the numbering system.

Bibliographical Note

Several works were consulted for the production of this chapter. These include: Martin Noth, *The Old Testament World* (Philadelphia: Fortress, 1966); Nahum M. Sarna, *Genesis*, Jewish Publication Society Torah Commentary (Philadelphia: Jewish Publication Society, 1989); Norman C. Habel, *The Book of Job: A Commentary*, Old Testament Library (Philadelphia: Westminster, 1985); and Arthur Weiser, *The Psalms: A Commentary*, Old Testament Library (Philadelphia: Westminster, 1962).

What It Really

Says: The Meaning of a Text Through Time

Sometimes one hears someone say he or she is going to look up a passage in the Bible to see what it really says. There is a notion that finding the "real" meaning of the text is as simple as finding the verse and taking the literal meaning as understood at the moment in which the text is read. This behavior often entails a translation of the biblical text as well, so there is already the understanding of the translator in the passage read standing between the reader and the meaning of the Bible. However, the words on the page of the Bible may or may not tell the reader what the tradition, the faith community, or the original author really meant by those words.

The meaning of any given biblical text has changed through time and within the religious traditions in which it has been used. The manners by which the words of any passage of the Bible have been understood change rapidly and in several different directions. Though there usually are regulations on how the text is to be read in any given religious community, even such directions cannot keep the meaning from changing slightly as different people read the same text. However, authoritative readings of scripture have appeared and been accepted through the ages. Here we wish to look at the history of readings made of one verse of one psalm. Psalm 82:1 provides a variety of interpretations by which the changes in understanding may be compared.

The Author's Verse

Psalm 82 reflects a religious world in which there had been a pantheon of gods in the religious cult of Judah, but now there was to be only the one God. Dates suggested for the composition of the poem range from the twelfth to the third centuries B.C.E., although scholarly opinion now tends toward accepting it as a product either of the Reform of Josiah (±622 B.C.E.) or the Babylonian exile (587–538 B.C.E). The author of the psalm believes that the gods who used to have control over the world, under the direction of the supreme deity, God, have misused their positions and therefore are being relieved of those positions by God, who will now take over sole rule of the world.

The author has chosen to use a series of puns, plays on words, repetition of sounds, and poetic structuring devices to produce a short, but clear poem. The use of the Hebrew word *elohim* for both "God" and "gods" plays a recurring part in the theme of the psalm. That the word *elohim* literally means both "God" and "gods" is useful for the poet's purposes; however, the word also can mean "mighty." The author used a common enough Northwest Semitic phrase, *adat-el,* to describe the group of deities; as the author composed the text the phrase meant the assembly of deities, those who serve under the supreme deity of the Northwest Semitic people's pantheon, the god El. Now, the name *El* also means "god" or "God" and can, in noun constructions such as this, simply denote "divine." What is clear in the passage is that this is the divine council of deities. The councils of deities are well attested in the myths throughout the ancient Near East, and the notion of a divine assembly appears in Judah (in the biblical texts) as well as among Judah's and Israel's neighboring countries.

Literally rendered within a world view that understood the universe to be ruled by a pantheon, the verse would read:

> God stands up
> In the assembly of El
> In the midst of the gods He judges.

This reflects a deity of the highest authority arising in the divine council to make a statement to the assembled gods. In this psalm the statement is a condemnation of their behavior, which has favored the wicked and crushed the poor and powerless. For these improprieties the supreme deity judges them unfit to govern (there is a pun on the word *shaphat,* which means both "to govern" and "to judge"). The punishment is death (deities in the ancient Near East could die, and improper behavior on the part of gods was subject to punishment from superior deities in the pantheon). The poem ends with the populace demanding that God rule the entire earth alone (with no minor deities).

This is a literal translation of the most common meaning of the words used in the poem. It is, however, not really a translation of the text as it was understood in the Bible. At no time in the history of the Book of Psalms as sacred text did the community believe in a pantheon for Judah. So, this translation is the meaning of the individual song written for the very end of the Judean temple cult or the very earliest Jewish worship after the Babylonian exile, but it is the meaning of the verse before it was considered part of the Bible.

The Book of Psalms' Verse

The Book of Psalms is a compilation of several independent songs that were collected over a period of time during the existence of the Second Temple. The collection as a whole has its own theological positions, and among these are the insistence that there is only one God, that this God is responsible for the entire world, and that God sees to it that good people are rewarded and evil people are punished. The fact that Psalm 82 was included in the collection shows that the translation of the second "elohim" in the verse as "gods" was not the understanding of the compiler of the Book of Psalms. However, it is clear that the Book of Psalms recognized that there were angels (literally "messengers") who served God in ruling the world, and it is known that in some of the Dead Sea Scrolls the word "elohim" was used for "angels." From this it is fairly clear to see that the meaning of the Hebrew word "elohim" had been adapted from meaning all divine beings to refer to only the single lowest level of such beings, the divine messengers. Since, in the theology of the editors of the Book of Psalms, there could be only one God, the assembly could not be assumed to be the gods who belonged to El; therefore, the word "el" must be taken as the generic word for "god," understood, of course, to refer to the only God. Thus, at that time the verse was considered to refer to God's heavenly assembly of angels.

When the compilers of the Book of Psalms read the verse, they read:

> God stands up
> In the assembly of God
> In the midst of the angels He judges.

The rest of the psalm read much the same as it had when it was understood to refer to deities. Since angels were understood to rule parts of the world, especially the nations around Judea, these divine beings were being punished for allowing their peoples and nations to behave in an evil manner. Again, the punishment would be "to fall," a euphemism for death, such that God is called upon to rule the universe alone. The intent is clear: The world is a much better place with God ruling directly than it was when intermediates had control.

A Twist on the Verse Toward Enoch

By the second century B.C.E. there had developed a notion about "fallen angels" and Psalm 82 (along with Gen. 6:1–4; Isa. 14:12–17; and Ezek. 28:2–13) provided the biblical basis for the belief that a group of angels had revolted in heaven, causing God to throw them into the place of death (*sheol* was merely an underground abode of the dead in the time of ancient Israel and Judah; by New Testament times it had been replaced in theological thought with *hades* [English: "hell"], wherein these fallen angels were supposed to dwell with the evil dead).

The compiler of the Book of Psalms did not know about "fallen angels," a notion that would appear in theological speculation only at a later time than when the book was edited, but only knew of angels condemned to die. Yet, some persons reading this psalm by the first century B.C.E. could find demonic, fallen angels in it, and such is the way the material is used in the Book of Enoch (the book in the Ethiopian Orthodox Bible). So, while a translation of the psalm's verse for those persons reading in the "fallen angel" tradition would be exactly the same as that for the compilers of the Book of Psalms, the meaning was related to a wider understanding of the universe. For the author of the Book of Enoch and the traditions related to the "fallen angels" motif, the verse described not just the punishment of disobedient heavenly personnel, but the establishment of an entire mirror-image universe to the good ruling God with helpful angels in heaven, producing an evil destructive devil with malevolent fallen angels (read: demons) in hell. So we have the same translation exactly, but a very different meaning. For the Enochian tradition, this verse describes the moment at which the devil and the demons were tossed out of heaven into hell and the world was divided into two opposed camps, one good and one evil.

The Verse of the Greek-Speaking Jews in Alexandria

The Septuagint provides a glimpse of how the Jews in Alexandria, Egypt, read their Hebrew Psalm. The Greek of Psalm 82:1 reflects an understanding close to that of the original author. There are gods in this poem. Not only is the second "elohim" taken as a reference to the pantheon, but the "el" of the assembly is translated as "gods" and not "God." The assembly (*'adat*) is translated with *synagoge*, the word for congregation, and the final word for "to judge" becomes the word for settling disputes.

The translation for the Alexandrian Jewish community (or the translation of the Greek translation of the Hebrew) reads:

> God stands
> In the Congregation of the gods
> In the middle of the gods He settles disputes.

It was the Greek text, with its subtle changes in the meaning of the verse, that was used by the early church. Indeed, it is clear from John 10:34 (which quotes Ps. 82:6) that the Christian author of the Gospel understood the second "elohim" (gods/God) to refer to humans and then goes on to posit that the use of "elohim" in the singular (as when it refers to God) may be used by the church for Jesus.

The Rabbis Read the Verse

The Book of Psalms only became a Bible text when it was incorporated into the canon of authoritative books. For both Jewish and Christian traditions that point came in the process of debate during the first four centureis C.E. The Talmud was closed by its being written down ca. 400 C.E., which essentially closed the canon of the Tanak for Jewish tradition. The understanding of the books that were accepted into the ranks of sacred books (those which "defile the hands" as the rabbinic tradition referred to canonical works) was the understanding of the rabbis who made the decisions. What the rabbis thought Psalm 82:1 meant is recorded in the Talmud, and this has been considered the official biblical meaning of the verse for the Jewish tradition until this day.

The "assembly of God" was understood to refer to the Jewish people in the general designation "Israel." However, the second "elohim" was understood as a variation of the meaning "mighty," meaning "those who are mighty." This was understood to be a reference to the human judges who passed sentence on the behavior of the Jewish community. Therefore the verse was read:

God stands up
In Israel
In the midst of the judges He judges.

The Jewish meaning of the text clearly set it on the human level. The corrupt judges are not slain, however; they are simply reminded by the punishment phrase that they are human just like everyone else and therefore are to handle their office in a properly merciful manner, remembering that there is a heavenly Judge who rules the entire universe, the judges included.

The Verse as Read by Origen

Undoubtedly the most gifted biblical scholar of the ancient church was Origen of Alexandria (ca. 185–ca. 254 C.E.). He worked out a method for interpreting scripture on three levels: literal, historical, and moral. For him the last was the most important, but he also wrote concerning the other meanings. Through his students he became the most influential biblical commentator in the early church, even though he himself was excommunicated posthumously for theological reasons.

Though his commentary on the Psalms has been lost, he makes enough references to the psalm in other works that the verse in question can be reconstructed according to his literal meaning. Using the Alexandrian Greek biblical text, Origen sees the "congregation of gods" as a reference to the false gods of the non-Jewish, non-Christian peoples. These, he explains, were the "fallen angels" who were tossed out of heaven to become demons (the tradition that produced Enoch was popular in the early church generally). For him the verse read:

God stands
In the assembly of demons
In the midst of demons He judges.

This provides one interpretation of the meaning of the verse in early Christian scholarship, but it was not the only one.

Augustine Reads the Verse

At roughly the time that the African Council at Carthage was deciding that the Book of Psalms was a canonical text, Augustine, Bishop of Hippo (354–430 C.E.) wrote his commentary on the Psalms. Augustine was dependent on the Latin translation of the

Greek text, in which the only major change was the return of the original "el" to a singluar "God" which precluded treating the last word of the phrase "'adat-el" as referring to "demons," "gods," or any other plural collective.

Since Augustine had developed a theology in which the persons of the Trinity could be discerned in the passages of the Bible, the Bishop could tell that the first reference to God was a reference to the Second Person of the Trinity, that is: Christ. It was his understanding that all descriptions of God that posited human attributes to the deity in fact meant Christ. The assembly of God was taken by Augustine to mean the synagogue of Israel. Already, in earlier Christian interpretation, the Greek "synagoge" had been associated with those people of God who met in worship in a community they themselves called "the synagogue." Augustine simply adopted this interpretation of the verse and used, as did the rabbis, the term "Israel" to refer to the religious community of Jews as a whole. However, Augustine understood the "mighty" at the end of the verse also to refer to the Jews who worshiped in the synagogue. Thus, for Augustine, the psalm became an allegory for the turning of God away from the Jews and toward the Christians. Augustine would have read the text as:

> Christ stands
> In the synagogue of Israel
> In the midst of the Jews He judges.

For those Christians who were deciding that the Book of Psalms was included in the Christian canon, Psalm 82 had become a parable about the shift of God's favor, a topic central to several parables in the New Testament, especially in the Gospel of Matthew. It cannot be stressed too heavily that this theological position has led to horrific actions by Christians against Jews in the millennium-and-a-half since Augustine. Although it is clear that Augustine's reading of the text was widespread in his day and for a millennium following was the accepted understanding of the passage in Western Christian circles, it is not an interpretation that can be accepted in the modern church, although there are Christian groups that still hold this position and would accept Augustine's reading as authoritative. That Christians see themselves as joining Jews among the chosen of God, rather than replacing them, has become ever more common in the last half of the twentieth century.

Martin Luther and Psalm 82:1

The Protestant reformer Martin Luther (1483–1546) dealt with the psalms more than once. In his commentaries on the Psalms he displays his education in the Augustinian monastic academies from which he came. So, for example, the first reference to God in this passage is understood to be Jesus as the First Person of the Trinity. However, the "assembly of God" denoted the Christian community for Luther rather than the community of Jewish worshipers. The final "mighty" (for Luther was translating from the Hebrew text, not Greek or Latin, although we can see how interpretations from those working with Greek and Latin texts have influenced his reading of the Hebrew) was understood as the civil officials of the Christian state, that is, those who hold authoritative positions. In this manner Luther reads the verse as:

> Jesus stands up
> In the Christian community
> In the midst of the officials He judges.

Luther, and John Calvin along with him, read the psalm as a call from Christ to take a stand in the face of corruption in the Christian world. In the course of interpreting the meaning of the psalm, the Protestant reformers saw a biblical injunction to confront not only the civil leaders of their society, but also the church hierarchy. The psalm meant for them that God had called for the overthrow of those in power so that the true rule of God could be established. Of course, the Protestants assumed they were bringing in that reign of God referred to at the end of the psalm.

Liberation Theology and the Verse

Psalm 82 has been a popular poem in the thought of liberation theologians from various backgrounds. Late-twentieth-century theological thought has been heavily influenced by a uniting of the theologies of the absolute authority of God and the theology of the cross. These are then interpreted through the economic and sociological thought of Marxist philosophy and social activist Christianity. The origins of the biblical interpretation of the liberation theologians is essentially mid-century European adapted to the immediate contexts of Latin America, Africa, East Asia, Southeast Asia, and Oceania; increasingly the practical nature of this theology has been adopted not only by American theologians involved in the struggles of the cultural underclass, but also in seminary theological theory.

Essentially, the poem is understood by Liberation interpretation as a statement that God's first concern is with the poor, impoverished, and powerless of society (who are those especially in the concern of God) and that those in positions of power have oppressed and abused those under their authority. The judging of the powerful is taken as a condemnation of the pursuit of power. The call for God to rule the entire earth in place of the rulers of the world is taken as a demand for total equality and an end to privilege. A generic reading of the meaning of the verse within this tradition would appear as:

> God stands
> Among the devout
> In the midst of the empowered He condemns.

Here the devout would be the poor, powerless, and oppressed, while those being condemned are the empowered, wealthy leaders who have oppressed the powerless.

The section of the psalm listing the abuses of the powerless by the powerful are understood to be descriptions of the general nature of power itself. The punishment by God is not assumed to necessarily entail the death of the powerful, only that they become one with everyone else; which is to call for a complete realignment of the structure of society. The final call for God alone to rule the entire earth is understood to mean that all humans are equal before God and that all persons are equally required to fulfill the mutual aid of God's community.

It Really Means?

This series of options for understanding one verse of one psalm should display the problem of taking seriously anyone who begins a sentence with, "What the Bible *really* says is...." The Bible has said many things to different people. The meaning read from the texts changes depending upon which religious community one happens to be reading the text from (no Orthodox Jewish reader will ever read Psalm 82:1 as referring to Christ, nor should they). It also depends on what time period in one's religious tradition one assumes the normative interpretation for scripture was set in (if one believes the author's intention is always correct, Psalm 82:1 demands a belief in a pantheon of gods; not very likely to catch on in either Christian or Jewish circles). And the meaning depends on the cultural context of the reader of the verse itself (Liberation Theology readings have always emphasized the context of Bible reading, and it is a matter of significance for understanding what the Bible actually says to individuals).

The final conclusion from a study like this must be that Bible texts bear numerous meanings. Different Jewish and Christian communities have understood the very same passages in very different ways through time and throughout the world. Different denominations in the Christian Protestant tradition of North America alone have taught and passed down numerous different readings of the same verses; each is taken as authoritative within its own tradition, but not necessarily having any status beyond that denomination. The Bible retains its status as a sacred text only within a worshiping community and, to a large extent, it is the community, and the tradition borne by the witnesses to the faith, that really do determine what the text says. The texts say many things, really.

Questions for Reflection and Discussion

1. What sort of problems might develop if it was decided that the real meaning of any biblical text was that of the person who wrote the text in the first place?

2. Do the understandings held of the Bible by other traditions help one understand those of one's own community?

3. Does everyone understand the difference between reading the Bible for the meaning of the individual books and for the meaning of the biblical text?

4. Why is the Augustinian interpretation of Psalm 82 a serious problem for the church?

5. There is also "reader response" interpretation, by which the meaning derived by any given person simply reading a passage, with or without background, is the meaning for that person. How does each one read and understand Psalm 82 in their own words?

Bibliographical Note

This chapter is adapted from two articles: Lowell K. Handy, "Sounds, Words and Meanings in Psalm 82," *Journal for the Study of the Old Testament* 47 (1990), pp. 51-66; and Lowell K. Handy, "One Problem Involved in Translating to Meaning: An Example of Acknowledging Time and Tradition," *Scandinavian Journal of the Old*

Testament 10 (1996), pp. 16-27. A trio of books that might interest readers on the various meanings that have been read from biblical texts: On Exodus: Brevard S. Childs, *The Book of Exodus: A Critical, Theological Commentary*, Old Testament Library (Philadelphia: Westminster, 1974); Jewish reflections on the Joseph narrative: James L. Kugel, *In Potiphar's House: The Interpretive Life of Biblical Texts* (Cambridge, Mass.: Harvard University Press, 1994); on the Gospel presentations of Jesus: John Bowden, *Jesus: The Unanswered Questions* (Nashville: Abingdon, 1989). Two recent interesting volumes on the historical encounter between cultures and particular texts in the Bible can be found regarding Eden: Jean Delumeau, *History of Paradise: The Garden of Eden in Myth and Tradition* (New York: Continuum, 1995); and Noah's Flood: Davis A. Young, *The Biblical Flood: A Case Study of the Church's Response to Extrabiblical Evidence* (Grand Rapids: Eerdmans, 1995)

Some THOUGHTS
About Translating

Very few laypersons read the Bible in its original languages. We are dependent on translations made by people who know the ancient languages of Hebrew, Aramaic, and Koine Greek (the New Testament was written in the common Greek spoken by the general population, not the classical Greek of the Golden Age of Greek literature; the common language is called "Koine Greek" to distinguish it from classical Greek) as well as the modern language into which the translation is being made (for the purposes of this chapter, the translation language will be assumed to be English; all aspects of translating affect all other languages). Portions of the Bible have been translated into more languages than any other work and the process continues. But translations are never the same as the text that was translated. The problems entailed in translating the biblical text are numerous and complicated. Only a few complications can be mentioned here, but they will suffice to demonstrate the magnitude of the effort.

Before One Begins
The first thing a translator needs to determine is what Bible is to be translated. Usually this is not a decision that is debated for very long. Protestants usually translate their own canon, Catholics theirs, Assyrian Orthodox Church scholars theirs, and so forth.

Indeed, many translators have their project determined for them by the publisher paying for the work. Denominational presses usually print books for their own members, though the National Council of Churches has taken to producing translations for numerous mainline American Churches.

There are other considerations, however. Many Protestant Bibles include the Protestant Apocrypha (the Roman Catholic Deuterocanon); many Roman Catholic Bibles have traditionally contained the Catholic Apocrypha (remember this is not the Protestant Apocrypha, which is a constituent part of the Catholic Bible); modern East Syriac New Testaments usually include the New Testament books contained in the Catholic canon, but not in their own; and so forth. Even after the biblical books for translation have been determined, some thought has to be given to the texts of the individual books. If the canon to be translated includes Tobit, there are two versions of the story, both acceptable as canonical, but one has to be chosen for any given Bible. Other books entail determining which reconstruction of the Hebrew, Aramaic, and (especially) Greek text is to be used. Usually, these days, the Masoretic Text of the Old Testament is used for the Tanak or the Old Testament where it has books in the canon being translated. Aside from the books of the Hebrew Bible, however, there is a large choice of possible manuscripts to choose from for all other books.

The translator must also determine what point along the tradition of transmitting the Bible the English version is going to represent since the meaning read from the same words changes. Usually, the modern translation reflects a point in understanding the text between its original authorship and its becoming officially listed as canonical. While some Bible scholars prefer to attempt to translate the original meaning, they often avoid the more obviously polytheistic, highly polemical, or theologically questionable meanings that appear in the clear manuscript sentences. Or, as in the case of the Song of Songs, where the text can be rendered literally with a highly erotic vocabulary, they purposefully translate those words bearing multiple meanings in a fashion suitable for public religious recitation; though, of course, there are those scholars who prefer the most unorthodox readings possible. Choosing the historical point in time of the reading of the Bible will determine what certain words are to mean, since the definitions of ancient words changed through time as much as modern language changes; the translator needs to know what the meanings were at the time of the proposed reading used for translation.

How Close a Translation?

The text of any translated Bible will fall somewhere between a strict translation and a paraphrase. Translations attempt to replicate the text of the original languages in English. The closer the English is to the literal text, the more difficult it is to read. Greek syntax is not English syntax and Hebrew noun-verb order is the reverse of English. This is the first sentence of Genesis if written dead literally, word for word:

> In head created gods the heavens and the earth and the earth was chaotic and void and darkness upon face of chaoswater and spirit of gods hovering upon face of the waters and said gods, "Be light!" and was light.

Which may well explain why translators avoid word-for-word translations. Instead the usual attempt has been to produce as close a translation as possible using standard English.

A problem arises when one has to deal with things like idioms (phrases that bear a meaning other than the literal understanding of the words; for example, the American English phrase "warm hearted" does not mean the person is suffering from a fever in the cardiac muscles) or cultural phenomena. Do you translate the Hebrew idiom literally as "his nostril burned" or the English standard: "he was angry" because that is what the Hebrew means in English terms? Recently, the notion of "dynamic equivalence" has taken cultural phenomena (such as the times of day) and insisted that they be translated into modern terminology. So, in Matthew 20:3 the Greek says the landowner went out "about the third hour," which comes out in the *New Revised Standard Version* as "about nine o'clock." The translation of "third hour" as "nine o'clock" is argued to convey meaning to the English reader who would not understand time keeping in the Roman Empire; however, it is not really a translation of the text, or even of the meaning of the text, only an attempt to have the text make sense to the modern reader. In like manner, the current project to create a Bible that does away with the traditional English default to male terms in the language attempts to translate the Greek of the New Testament to reflect the inclusiveness inherent in the terms used by the Greek authors themselves; so far only the New Testament has been published: *The New Testament of the Inclusive Language Bible.*

One way to deal with the difference in languages is the paraphrase option. Most scholars despise paraphrases on principle.

However, most laity like texts that read easily and carry meaning without the reader having to ponder what the text is trying to say. The most successful recent paraphrase was *The Living Bible: Paraphrased,* which bore the clear stamp of its translator, Kenneth Nathaniel Taylor, who changed some texts to suit his own theological positions. There is nothing particularly wrong with this, however; it is clear that the changes were made because the author of the book believed that was the real meaning of the text. The entire Bible appears in a readable, if sometimes strange, edition. A less successful, but even more paraphrased Bible was produced by the Readers Digest Company wherein the text was actually shortened to what the editors believed was its basic content.

This brings us to the tradition of "translating to meaning" which, in fact (despite contentions to the contrary), is a combination of translating and paraphrasing; it is the method by which most modern Bible translations are produced. Here one takes the most reasonable meaning conveyed by a text to translate a given passage; the first sentence in Genesis so translated could read:

> When God began to create heaven and earth, the earth was chaotic and void and there was darkness over the surface of the chaos-waters; while the spirit of God hovered over the surface of the waters, God said, "Let there be light!" and there was light.

This text is neither literal, nor paraphrased, but it is readable and a reasonable approximation of the meaning of the text.

The Translated Language

The style for the language of the translated edition has to be consistent. The entire Bible may be translated into a majestic form of the English language, the intent being for the text to be inspiring when read from the pulpit; this is one reason the King James Version has held on to the popular imagination of Protestant Christianity in the English speaking world, for though it may not always be accurate, it is unquestionably majestic. In the other direction, the Bible has been translated into common speech; one can think of the American Bible Society's *Good News Bible* or Clarence Jordan's *Cotton Patch Bible,* among numerous others, as serious attempts to put biblical text into the spoken language of the readers. Usually, the translator strives for a combination of reverential language and understandability.

English translations are numerous and need to be so if the intent of the translators is to make a Bible in the everyday speech of the readers. English is a language that spans the globe, and it is not the same in India, Kenya, or the United States as is it is in Great Britain (or even in Boston as in Atlanta, or in Edinburgh as in Canterbury). The community for which the translation is being made helps determine the form of the English to be used. The vocabularies of Hebrew or Greek and modern English may not be the same on certain terms; English translations tend to translate all the various types of Israelite priests as "priest," which does not convey the variety in the original; to the other extreme, English New Testaments often simply bring over titles from the Greek (or its Latin equivalents), assuming we all know the levels of Roman hierarchy (what was a "hekatontarches" [centurion] ?).

Vocabulary Problems

But one need not turn to the interaction of the two languages to find vocabulary problems that must be handled by the translators. Hebrew and Greek words carried several meanings, as do modern English words (quickly now, translate "row" into Spanish: is it *pelea* [a "quarrel"], *fila* [a "line"], or *llevar* [literally "to carry," used as "to row" a boat]). Words with many meanings can provide endless headaches to translators.

Returning to the opening sentence of Genesis, one of the recurring decisions that faces all translators is what to do with the phrase in Genesis 1:2, "ruah 'elohim." The Hebrew word *ruah* means "spirit," "wind," "breath," and even "the center of mental or moral reasoning." In addition, *'elohim* means "gods" in its basic declension; however, it means just as certainly "God," "divine," and "mighty." What this means is that a translator can legitimately put any of these combinations together and have a literal translation of the Hebrew phrase. So, some Bibles read "Spirit of God," others read "mighty wind," and still others have "breath of God." All are correctly and literally translated. One does not usually find "wind of the gods," or "divine center of mental or moral reasoning," not because the translations would be wrong for the phrase, but because they are not considered reasonable for the passage as a whole.

Often the cultural context of a term presents difficulties. Some characters come to see the infant Jesus in Matthew 2:1, 7; the Greek says they were *magoi.* Now, everyone who has ever studied ancient religions knows that the magi are a particular order of Zoroastrian priests, and Zoroastrianism was the official religion of Parthia, the great empire directly to the east of the Roman Empire (the religion is still alive and well, even in parts of the United States, usually referred to today as Parsiism). Yet, many Bibles translate the word as "wise men," or "astrologers" because, for Roman readers, the priestly status of the magi was unimportant (or even unknown), and these persons were known in the Roman Empire mostly for being highly educated and for knowing how to read the movements of the stars and constellations.

When the Bible texts turn to plays on words, the translators' problems multiply. How do you get a pun across in another language? The best translations of Lewis Carroll's Alice books are generally considered those that have written the text over entirely so the punning is retained but the content now conforms to the culture and language into which the translation has been made. The translator of a biblical pun, however, does not feel at liberty to simply exchange a similar pun from English into the text, since the meaning of the text itself must be retained.

How, then, does one translate a Hebrew text that says a human (Hebrew *adam*) was fashioned out of the ground (Hebrew *adamah*)? One could write that a "human" was fashioned out of "humus," but humus is not the same thing as ground. In a similar manner, while the Hebrew text produces a pun on what the first humans were not wearing (*'arummim*) in Genesis 2:25 with the description of the serpent in Genesis 3:1 (*'arum*), the English language simply does not have two words that sound almost alike but mean respectively "naked" and "clever." Without exception translators of this passage go for the meaning of the words and leave the notation of the word play to a footnote, if mentioned at all.

As is clear from the immediately preceding material, many words in the Bible have several meanings or can be translated with several different English words. For the sake of consistency many modern translators seek to use the same English word for the same Hebrew word wherever it appears in the book being translated or in the Bible as a whole. This system cannot be carried out everywhere and still make sense. When *'elohim* means "God" it comes with singular verbs or singular modifiers, but when it means "gods," the verbs and modifiers are plural; to choose singular or plural and to translate all instances consistently would make nonsense out of the noun-verb number correlation, not to mention the sense of the texts.

Certain conjunctions mean so many different things that to translate them consistently (or even at all in some instances) would read like madness. The Greek conjunction *kai* is the standard word for "and," "but," "also," "even," and a host of other English words (not to mention simply being at times the marker for the beginning of a new sentence) and to consistently translate *kai* as "and" would, in fact, be mistranslating the text. The Hebrew conjunction prefix "w" or "u" (they are the same letter in Hebrew) presents exactly the same situation with the addition that it is the usual introduction to a temporal clause (so needing then to be translated "then," "when" or "while"). But those translators who wish to be consistent are not just being simplistic in their endeavor; they wish to show how those different passages, using the same words, relate to each other throughout the Bible, and this cannot be demonstrated if the vocabulary changes from place to place in the translated texts.

Another solution to the problem of words with multiple meanings is to translate the words to fit whatever meaning is required in the individual passages where the word appears. This method provides a more precise translation of each occurrence of the word, but fails to allow the reader in English to recognize the use of the same word or phrase in different environments. If someone was using an English Bible and wished to search the text for the meaning of "angel," for example, she or he would have to know at the outset that Greek *angelos* (which technically would be transliterated [that is, converted to the English alphabet letter for letter] as *aggelos*; Greek "gg" is read as "ng") means both "angel" and "messenger"; New Testament translators use both English words to translate the same Greek word, usually depending on whether the translator assumes the character in the passage is heavenly or human. The reader is dependent on the translator's having made the right decision.

Yet another problem with translating words should be mentioned. Many Hebrew and Greek words cannot be translated into English by means of one English word. This is not just the case because suffixes provide possessive pronouns, but both biblical languages are gender-based. In order to translate the single word for "she said" from either language, two words have to be used in English; there is no other way to get both aspects of the single word across into English. The same applies to the words for the professions. If one wishes to convey the difference between male and female singers, for example, two English words need to be used, since the words in Hebrew or Greek bear the gender within themselves; on the other hand, English does have "prophetess" and "priestess," even if they sound a bit old-fashioned. However, there are reasons for not dividing out words on gender lines in translation. The prophetess Huldah should not be distinguished from the prophet Jeremiah on the basis of the gender of their office; if we use different terms for them it can be, and has been, implied that they are in some way engaged in different activities as conveyers of the word of God, although it is clear from the biblical texts that the authors assumed that what Huldah did was the same thing as what Jeremiah did (or maybe she did it even better, given her use by King Josiah, but that's another matter for another study).

Sometimes the force of the original language is lost in translation. English language cannot replicate the form of the condemnation of David by Nathan in 2 Samuel 12:7, since Hebrew can make the whole statement in two words, *'attah ha'ish,* producing a short, biting damnation, but English needs four: "You are the man!" In the same manner, it is difficult to determine what the connotations of words were and how to convey them in English. Moreover, some words carried associations that cannot be conveyed by the English text; whereas the biblical disdain for "Babylon" has, more or less, carried through the New Testament and Christian traditions into common usage, the connotations surrounding "Moabite" are generally unknown to most readers of the Bible (Moabites were considered both enemies and objects of mirthful contempt by the authors of the Hebrew Bible), and this cannot be conveyed simply be making a translation of the word.

Finally, a comment on the English words themselves. The King James Version remains a popular translation, but much of the vocabulary of the Hebrew text from which it was translated was simply unknown to the translators in their time. Being unaware of the animal life of the ancient world, the scholars came up with the translation "unicorn" for what we now tend to translate as "wild ox" (check Numbers 23:22; 24:8; Deuteronomy 33:17; Job 39:9,10; Psalm 22:21; 29:6; 92:10; Isaiah 34:7); there are no unicorns in the biblical texts. This is not just a problem for older translations; much of the vocabulary of the Book of Job remains uncertain. As knowledge of the meanings of ancient vocabulary grows, changes in translations will continue to need to be made. Other words have changed meaning within English usage. "Suffer" seldom is used for "to allow" in common speech; however, Matthew 19:14, Mark 10:14, and Luke 18:16 in the King James Version have Jesus use an expression common enough in the time of the translators: "suffer the little children"; this simply meant to allow them. "Suffer" carried two meanings then (Mark 9:12 uses it in the modern sense), but has one now, and translations need to reflect this shift in English usage.

Poetry

Poetry provides even more problems. As in modern poetry, the full effect of a poem in the ancient world was related to the manner in which the words, meter, and sounds came together when recited. Though rhyme, mercifully, is seldom a part of biblical poetry, either Hebrew or Greek, the poetic norms of the two languages determine the form of the text. Should the translator attempt to replicate the exact poetic norms for a language that has no such poetic traditions? The results may well sound like mush in translation.

Moreover, Hebrew poetry traditionally was written on scrolls in the same fashion as prose, one line after another filling up the margins. Early New Testament manuscripts printed Greek poetry in the texts in the same fashion. Poetry in English is written by the lines of the verses forming a series of short segments that do not usually reach the right margin but have a common margin to the left. Indeed, when modern editors print Hebrew or Greek biblical texts for Western scholars, they tend to print it in Western verse formation so that the poetry is distinguished from the prose around it. However, that is not the way the texts are found in manuscript, and some poetry may not have been printed by the editors as poetry, or maybe some prose was printed as poetry by mistake.

Since Hebrew poetry has as its basic feature a structure known as "parallelism," printing the prose-like manuscript texts in English poetic-type formulas is pretty simple. One verse in parallelism with another says a very similar thing in different words, which slightly change and advance the poem, but it is difficult to find English words that will carry the same meaning as the Hebrew. This leads to the end that many readers get tired of reading texts that seem to be constantly saying the same thing twice or three times over, since it is not a form of poetry to which they are accustomed. In Greek it is occasionally hard to tell whether one is dealing with a poetic or prose text, since highly rhetorical prose tends to sound a great deal like poetry. It is generally agreed at this time that Paul quotes from a hymn of his churches in Philippians

2:6–11, though there are scholars who insist that it is merely very well-crafted prose.

Names

Everyone knows the names of the major biblical figures. However, the names most Christians in the English-speaking world are familiar with are the English formulations of the names as they appear in the Bible. Many of the names in English Bibles are close transliterations of the names as they appear in the original textual languages, but some names have been adapted to the norms of English usage. Should the translator try to use the name that appears in the text or one that has become standard in English? A few examples will demonstrate.

Moses is certainly one of the most famous characters in the biblical tradition, but he is always called "Mosheh" in Hebrew. Sha'ul was the name given to numerous men who appear in the genealogy lists of Chronicles, but in English the first King of Israel becomes Saul, while the others tend to remain Sha'ul so that the English reader would not know how common the name actually had been. Would you recognize the three major prophets' names if they came and introduced themselves: Yesha'yahu, Yirmeyahu, and Yehzeqel (Isaiah, Jeremiah, and Ezekiel respectively)? The "y" sounds of Hebrew and Greek have usually been transformed into English "j" sounds, so Hebrew Eliyahu becomes Elijah and Greek Iesous (pronounced yasus) becomes Jesus.

As translators deal with names moving from the Hebrew Old Testament to the Greek New Testament, it is not only the English that has to be considered, but also the relation between the Hebrew form of names and the Greek form of the same names. Iesous, is after all, the Greek form of the Hebrew name Yehoshua'; no doubt Mary (Mariam, the Greek of Hebrew Miryam) and Joseph (Yosef in both Greek and Hebrew, though pronounced in both Yosaf)] named their child Yehoshua', knowing it was the name of the biblical character that we find in our Bibles called Joshua. Should Jesus be translated as Joshua because that was his name as commonly rendered in English, or should the tradition of referring to him with the English form of the Greek translation of his name (Jesus) be retained? There is in the New Testament a letter by James. However, if you look this letter up in a Greek manuscript you will discover that it is by Iakobos. The name James in English is used for the Greek form for the Hebrew name Ya'aqob, which itself is rendered into English as Jacob. Finally, most translators use Moses for the leader of the exile wherever the name appears, but the Greek New Testament form of the name is not the Hebrew "Mosheh," but the Greek form "Mouses" (pronounced Mausas).

Any translation of the Bible that intends to produce a Christian Bible with both testaments has to determine how they are going to handle the names. Consistency will produce a Bible in which the persons with the same name may be understood as related through their names, but readers have come to refer to Jesus not as Joshua and certainly not as Yehoshua'.

Final Cautionary Notation

For the reader using a translation of the Bible it is necessary to understand that there are numerous problems entailed in making a translation. It is always necessary for one using a translation to have some idea as to whether they are reading a translation, a paraphrase, or a combination of these forms. It is also wise to have some idea as to what the purpose of the Bible translation was in the eyes of those who produced it. Scholarly literal translations usually are not suitable for lectionary readings, official translations for worship services often carry the interpretive stamp of the denomination using them, and all translations fail to replicate the Hebrew, Aramaic, and Greek texts, but only approximate them. It is wise, when seeking to understand the meaning of a biblical text from translations, to gather two or more different translations and compare the passages being studied as they appear in the various Bibles.

Questions for Reflection and Discussion

1. Why do professors at the undergraduate level of college suggest that their students check with several different translations when determining the meaning of a particular biblical passage?

2. What difference does it make if you translate the phrase in Genesis as "Spirit of God" or "mighty wind," since they are both accurate literal translations?

3. Can you think of English words that have more than one meaning that would be a problem to translate consistently into another language (like: "like" which means "as" and "fondness for" and "enjoy")?

4. Should Bibles use the names of the persons in a fashion as near to the original names as possible, or adapt to changing forms in the texts themselves, as well as English standard usage?

5. Anyone who has ever had to translate anything knows what troubles arise in attempting to get specialized meanings across; what other problems can you imagine pertain to translating, and how would these relate to translating the Bible?

Bibliographical Note

Use was made of Troy Martin, "Time and Money in Translation: A Comparison of the Revised Standard Version and the New Revised Standard Version" *Biblical Research* 38 (1993), pp. 55-73, in preparing this chapter. Still the most useful introduction to the whole enterprise of Bible translation remains: Eugen A. Nida and Charles R. Taber, *The Theory and Practice of Translation, Helps for Translators*, 8 (Leiden: E. J. Brill, 1974). Surveys of English translations may be found in Sakae Kubo and Walter F. Specht, *So Many Versions? Twentieth-Century English Versions of the Bible*, revised and enlarged edition (Grand Rapids: Zondervan, 1983); and Jack P. Lewis, *The English Bible from KJV to NIV: A History and Evaluation*, 2nd edition (Grand Rapids: Baker Book House, 1991).

AUTHORITY AND BIBLE READING

HOW IS ONE TO KNOW WHAT THE BIBLICAL TEXTS ARE SUPPOSED TO mean? Different religious traditions within Judaism and Christianity have different answers to that question. The authority of the text of the Bible itself varies by tradition as well. While each individual sect or denomination develops its own specific regulations for understanding the meaning of the Bible, some general comments concerning interpretive authority can be made.

Jewish Traditional Interpretation

Usually Jewish Bible interpretation can be divided into one of four traditional approaches. The plain sense meaning of a text (*peshat*) is considered the obvious level of meaning, open to any reader. A text may be interpreted as being an allusion (*remez*) to some teaching found at another part of scripture or in the Talmud. Some moral teaching might be discerned in the text that is not obvious and this manner of reading a text is sermonic (*derush*) allowing many acceptable interpretations. Finally, there is mystical interpretation (*sod*). All of these traditional interpretations have their origins in the Talmud.

Talmud

For Orthodox and Conservative communities within Judaism the definitive source for understanding the Tanak has always been the discussions of biblical meaning by the rabbis during the Period of the Tannaim (from ±100 B.C.E. to ±200 C.E.). "Tannaim" means "repeaters," referring to those who recited the "Oral Torah." It is believed in Orthodox Jewish tradition that the central arguments of the debates concerning the meaning of scripture were memorized and passed down by the disciples of the great biblical exegetes within the Pharasaic rabbinic schools. However, the commentary on the biblical texts is believed to have had its origin with the giving of the Torah to Moses. It is said that the Oral Torah was passed on from God to Moses, to Joshua, to the Judges, to the prophets, to Ezra, to the assembly of the Great Synagogue; each link in the chain of tradition is understood to have memorized the true interpretation of the written Tanak and then passed it on to only one worthy to keep the tradition.

The most important quotations from some eighty rabbis (and scattered citations from about seventy others) were written down as the Mishnah in ±200 C.E. by tradition the compilation of the Mishnah was undertaken by Judah the Patriarch. The Mishnah itself is ordered under six topics, which are then discussed with regard to the regulations and allowances concerning each as found in the Bible (as well as in Jewish interpretive tradition). The six topics are:

> Agriculture
> Appointed Times
> Women
> Damages
> Holy Things
> Purities

Each topic in turn is investigated along three levels of Jewish social life: (1) the interests of priests in matters concerning what is and is not holy, (2) the interests of scribes in keeping correctly the text and interpretation of the Tanak, and (3) the interests of the common population in how best to conduct their lives. The six topics, as dealt with in the Mishnah, are subdivided into a total of sixty-three "tractates," which expand on individual questions raised by the rabbis with regard to the major topics.

The rabbis had much more to say about the proper interpretation of the biblical tradition than was recorded in the Mishnah. They also had comments about the correct understanding of the Mishnah itself. Some of these additional observations were deemed authoritative themselves and were, in turn, collected into a commentary on the Mishnah called the Gemara. The Mishnah and Gemara together were compiled as the Talmud ±400 C.E. There are two Talmuds . The more complete edition was compiled in the Jewish scholarly community residing in Mesopotamia and so became known as the Babylonian Talmud (or "Eastern Talmud"). A shorter, and less complete, Talmud was compiled in Roman Palestine and is known as the Palestinian Talmud (or "Western Talmud"). Each of the sixty-three tractates of the Mishnah receives its own Talmudic book, so there are sixty-three Tractates (or books) in a full set of the Talmud. Gemara was not provided for all sixty-three tractates of the Mishnah; therefore, for those Mishnah texts lacking commentary, the Talmud supplies only the Mishnah, though sometimes a few short notes beyond the text of the Mishnah appear. It was the policy of the editors of the Talmud to record not only the positions that were accepted by the majority of rabbis, but also the opinions of the minority, thereby saving for posterity debates over meaning of scripture.

The Talmudic texts provide Jewish scholars a firm basis on which to determine the relevance of the biblical (and Talmudic) traditions for new social, political, and religious situations. For a talmudic scholar the study of the Talmud is begun at an early age, and the finest scholars are expected not only to know the Tanak by heart, but also the sixty-three tractates of the Talmud, and be able to relate the teachings of all of these to each other on any given topic. Various titles have been used through the centuries for the most learned rabbis, but their names continue to be cited in Jewish debate. The decisions of authoritative rabbis on Talmudic discussions for modern questions (called "responsa") can be found in several Orthodox and Conservative Jewish periodicals.

The Two Types of Interpretation

Since Hellenistic times, the Tanak has been open to interpretations as to its meaning by Jewish scholars who have learned the skills of proper investigation. Two general methodologies provided the arguments within the Talmud. The more serious investigation of sacred scripture is done by norms that are called "halakah." Those engaged in halakic research deal with the legal, moral, and social norms derived from the biblical texts. The Torah provides the base on which discussion is to be carried out, but the Talmudic texts provide the lens through which the Torah is to be read. The rules for halakic investigation are standard logical progressions of a legal nature, that is, how to adapt one attested case to another unattested but similar case. The responsa written by halakic scholars are to be taken seriously and incorporated into the daily life of the practicing Jew of the tradition in which the rabbi is recognized (just as among the clergy of Christian denominations, not all rabbis are recognized as authoritative among the divisions of Judaism). The other method of interpreting texts is known as "haggadah." The regulations for this form of biblical reading are much more lax, ranging from literary understandings to rather strange reconstructions of the text (probably the most unusual, if most interesting, is the system by which the letters of the Hebrew alphabet may be substituted with the numbering system, which uses the same symbols, to produce different words having the same numerical value). Haggadic interpretation has been popular since biblical times and continues to be so. By making use of the rules, one may fill in parts of stories in the Bible that do not appear in the texts themselves. The creative adaptations of biblical stories provide a large collection of variations on Bible narratives. These various readings have been considered important enough to treat with respect and to pass down in the teaching tradition, but no one is required to believe or obey material derived from the haggadic method of reading the Bible.

Much of the work of the medieval Jewish commentators involved both halakic and haggadic interpretation, and many of their works have become almost as central for Jewish Bible study as is the Talmud. However, Rabbi Solomon ben Isaac (usually referred to as Rashi, 1040–1105 C.E.) developed a literal, rational system of interpretation of the clear meaning of biblical passages. His concern for grammar and the force of narrative integrity produced a series of commentaries that dealt with entire books, not just passages or individual texts. His method of reading the Tanak along literal lines remains to this day a normative understanding of biblical texts in all Jewish scholarship.

Orthodox Christian Interpretation

Orthodox Christianity is defined by its conscious desire to retain the early forms of the church and the local nature of the individual Christian community. The interpretation of the biblical texts varies by Orthodox tradition, but the basic theory of interpretation remains constant throughout the orthodox communions.

Early Church Writers

For most churches of the Eastern Christian traditions, it is believed that the Seventh Ecumenical Council, held in Nice, France, in 787 C.E. (Second Nice Council) determined that the official Christian interpretation of the Bible was to be related to the authoritative writings by Christian biblical scholars to that point. Therefore, it is usual for biblical scholars in the Orthodox churches to begin any scholarly Bible interpretation by reading the works of Christian writers from the first eight centuries of the church.

Christianity began already having a sacred scripture. The Torah and the Prophets provided Jesus with the basis of his teaching, and the church that came after him used its "Bible" not only to explain Jesus' teachings, but to explain Jesus himself. As the various local churches added to the Writings of their sacred scriptures, two testaments developed, one from prophetic authors (Old Testament) and one from apostolic authors (New Testament). In the face of the heretic Marcion's mid–second-century declaration that the Old Testament was of no significance (indeed he deemed it evil), the church insisted that both testaments were of equal validity. The question was how to read them with a proper understanding.

Two major schools of biblical exegesis developed in the church by the end of the second century C.E. in two of the earliest centers of Christianity. One school developed in Alexandria, Egypt, and was heir to a long Jewish tradition of careful allegorical interpretation (along the line of the numerous works of Philo of Alexandria, ca. 20 B.C.E.–ca. 50 C.E., who strove to show the philosophical beliefs of his Greek contemporaries as having all derived from the Hebrew Bible). The other school was centered in Antioch, Syria, where there developed a concern for basic human understanding of the literal written word. Orthodox churches have continued to use the writings of both schools as authoritative sources for Bible study to this day.

The Alexandrian School of biblical interpretation eventually predominated in all parts of the late–first-millennium Christian world, and was the method of exegesis that was adopted by biblical scholars of the Western church, thereby predominating in the Roman Catholic Church throughout the Middle Ages. Three levels of interpretation were understood to correspond to the three aspects of the human being: literal (=body), moral (=soul), spiritual (=spirit). Of these the least important was considered to be the literal. The surface meanings of the texts were understood to reflect historical events but were not generally considered to be terribly important for the Christian readers' edification or salvation. Rather, deeper reading provided allegorical interpretations that could be used by Christians in their own lives. Every passage (even every word) of scripture was believed to have these three levels of interpretation. It should be pointed out that sometimes the moral and spiritual meanings collapsed into one interpretation, and in some instances the literal meaning was regarded as not historical. Nonetheless, this system of reading biblical texts allowed numerous lessons to be drawn from any given passage, and in both Eastern and Western Christianity subdivisions of moral and spiritual allegorical interpretations would be devised.

For an example of the basic three-fold interpretation, we might look at Genesis 19. The story of Lot and the destruction of Sodom and Gomorrah may be read as a historical account of the divine destruction of wicked cities. The importance of the narrative, however, comes in the allegorical readings of the tale. As a spiritual allegory the story becomes reflective of the exodus narrative: Lot becomes the Law, Lot's wife becomes those who looked back to the days in Egypt and died in the wilderness, and Lot's daughters become the two capital cities of the two nations devoted to God and God's laws, Jerusalem and Samaria. Reading the same story as moral allegory internalized the tale so as to conform to the moral decisions of individuals; Lot becomes the human mind, which has left behind the concerns of the flesh (Lot's wife), but still must deal with overcoming pride and vanity (Lot's daughters).

The Antiochene School insisted on dealing with the Bible on a literal level. Its scholars dismissed the allegorical readings of the Alexandrian School as so much nonsense. The purpose of an exegete was understood to be that of making as clear as possible the meaning of the Bible within the realm of Orthodox Christian doctrinal theology. The scholarship from Antioch tends to be concise, dealing at length only with those passages of scripture where the meaning is obscure or where the literal sense of a passage appears at first glance to be unorthodox insofar as it might be read as not conforming to Orthodox theological decisions. Teaching the congregation the word of God was of central importance and, therefore, those who preached were held in high esteem and were urged to produce long expositions on particular passages, making them relevant to the Christian congregation.

While the interpretive methods of the Antiochene School were retained in the Eastern churches, the Western church associated the Antiochene movement with various heresies that developed in the area of Antioch (though unrelated to the central figures of the biblical school). The result has been that only in the Orthodox churches have the careful theological-historical interpretations of the early Antioch church been retained in the study of biblical meaning. These interpretations include the reading of the prophecies found in the Old Testament as foretellings of Christ and the church, which might not strike all modern Western Christians as being the actual meaning of the original prophecies.

Typology

Sometimes typology and allegory are confused. In the theory of the early church, typology was treated as its own method. In reality, typology and allegory were often conflated and confused. It was for the first millennium of Christianity, and remains in the Eastern churches, a popular method of reading biblical texts.

Christian use of typology is derived from the New Testament texts themselves, though the origins of this method of biblical interpretation derive from Jewish rabbis. In simple terms, the theory holds that the passages of the Bible may be read as signifiers of things yet to come. For example, Jewish exegetes before the rise of Christianity already read the tabernacle (the "type") of Moses as a prefiguration of the Temple (the "antetype") in Jerusalem.

In the New Testament the Book of Hebrews uses the figure of Moses as the "type" for the "antetype" Jesus. While Moses led his people out to God they did not believe and died, though God gave them spiritual drink (water from the rock) and spiritual food (manna falling from heaven). The author of Hebrews contends that, while Moses did these things, the events also and equally prefigured the coming of Jesus who would lead his people to life through the spiritual drink (wine/blood) and spiritual food (bread/body) of the eucharist. However, First Peter presents the most complicated typology in the New Testament by demonstrating that the flood of Noah prefigured Christian baptism, which relives the crucifixion and resurrection of Jesus and itself prefigures the resurrection of the one baptised (1 Peter 3:18b–22).

Typological readings of many texts have passed into Orthodox tradition, both as Bible study and art. The typological reading of Genesis 18:2 sees in the three men coming to Abraham not just three men, but a "type" of the Trinity that was to come to humanity with the advent of Jesus and the coming of the Holy Spirit. Likewise, the burning bush of Exodus 3:2 could be read as "that which held God yet was not destroyed by bearing God within"; in Orthodox theology this immediately brings up the notion of the "Bearer of God," who is Mary (she who bore Jesus, bore God in the second person of the Trinity). The Old Testament passages, then, carry much more meaning than simply the literal text, not to mention that any given text may prefigure any number of "antetypes." Orthodox icon painting includes numerous examples of typological biblical references.

Ethiopian Orthodox Church

The one Christian tradition that established an authoritative biblical exegesis outside the influence of Europe is that of the Christian church in Ethiopia. By its own tradition, the Ethiopian Empire was ruled by direct descendants of the Queen of Sheba and Solomon; with the origins of Christianity traced back to the eunuch of Acts 8:27–39. Archaeology has traced churches in the area to the fourth century. In any case, the church in Ethiopia was effectively cut off from the rest of Christendom with the rise of Islam early in the seventh century, but its biblical studies continued in their own tradition uninterrupted.

The study of the Bible is generally carried on orally, much as the rabbis and earliest Christians passed on their understanding of the scriptures. The authoritative interpretation of the biblical text is carried out by the memorization of the "and′mta" which comments on the passages of the various books of the Ethiopian Orthodox canon. The method of treating the passages can be traced to two traditions, one Orthodox Christian and one traditional African. The basis of all biblical meaning is found in the literal meaning of the text in a fashion showing clear connections to the Antioch School of interpretation. However, like other Eastern Orthodox traditions, the Ethiopian Orthodox make use of typological meanings in Bible narratives; and unlike most other Orthodox traditions, biblical study is generally kept separate from theological disputes. The regional indigenous wisdom traditions of Eastern Africa were brought to bear on the texts and have become part of the interpretation of the meaning of the biblical texts. Therefore, the logic of reading a literal text is not the logic of Greece (and Europe), but the logic of traditional Ethiopia (and East Africa). Allegory is allowed in the Ethiopian Orthodox Church, but never to the diminishment of the literal meaning of a text.

The Emperor Zarea-Yaeqob (seventeenth century, though the date is debated) attempted to confront a rise in heretical positions infiltrating the Ethiopian Orthodox Church from other religious communities (including other Christian communities) and from indigenous magic. In both attempts he was essentially successful; however, his handling of African magic based on petitions to African gods allowed worshipers to accept traditional names of deities as hidden names of God. In the long run this has led to an entire biblical tradition in the Ethiopian Orthodox Church of reading biblical texts with secret and magical meanings related to the traditional beliefs and customs of East Africa, though understood to have derived from Jesus and God. (This, it should be noted, is not significantly distinguishable from English Christians incorporating the decidedly pagan traditions of Easter eggs [Slavic] and Christmas trees [Germanic] into Christian practice with new Christian [and sometimes old pagan] meanings). Zarea-Yaeqob's insistence on the keeping of the Ten Commandments meant that services on Saturday (Sabbath) were continued.

To a large extent, the Ethiopian Empire, for good or ill, attempted to mold society to biblical culture. In the end this process was one that used the meaning of the Bible as that meaning was influenced by Antiochian, African, and Arabic traditions. This results in a unique biblical authority, yet one readily discernable as belonging to the larger Christian Bible-reading community in the West.

Roman Catholic Church

The "church in the West" meant the Church of Rome for a millennium. The seat of the Bishop of Rome provided a unifying and authoritative center for the Western church that the Eastern churches did not have. Therefore, there was more consistency in the biblical interpretations within the Roman Catholic tradition through the early Middle Ages than among the Orthodox churches.

Tradition and Development

For the Roman Catholic Church the authoritative reading of scripture has centered in the tradition of the teachings of the church and in the continuity of the faith. While the Bible has always been the foundation of Catholic thought, its official interpretation depends on the work of those whose life vocation was to discern its meaning for the use of the Christian community. In this regard, the traditional teaching of the church, properly recognized, and the concern for the lives of the parish populace, properly instructed, determine what the Bible means for the contemporary church. Traditionally, the Western church used the Alexandrian School's methodology for biblical interpretation throughout the Middle Ages. The interpretation of biblical texts was further subdivided into specialized types of spiritual and moral meanings. There were studies on the teachings from any given passage regarding Christ, the church, the final judgment, and the kingdom of Heaven. Whole systems of symbolic interconnections among passages were developed on the basis of these spiritual meanings of the texts.

However, two borrowings from contemporary medieval Islam and Judaism provided new directions for biblical interpretation in the medieval schools of the Roman Catholic Church. The one most usually identified with the High Middle Ages is the rise of scholasticism, based on the discovery of the works of Aristotle by Catholic scholars. The other was related to the incorporation of contemporary Jewish commentaries on the books of the Old Testament. The former would lead to the Thomistic philosophy common into the twentieth century in Catholic thought; the latter would lead directly to the Protestant Reformation.

Two Muslim scholars were most responsible for the introduction of the philosophy of Aristotle into Western Christian circles, Abu 'Ali al Hosain ibn 'Abdallah ibn Sina (usually called Avicenna, 980–1037) and Ibn Rushd (usually called Averroes, 1126–1198). In their philosophical studies they dealt with the question of the realm of intellect in the area of revealed truth (for them, the Qur'an) with regard to the relation of humans to God. While they both used Aristotle as their primary mentor, they both included the Neoplatonic philosophy that was popular at their time in Islamic philosophical circles. The works of both scholars were translated into Hebrew by Jewish scholars and from there into Latin. While much of the content in these Islamic works was found to be unacceptable by Catholic scholars, the writings of Aristotle were eagerly sought after and incorporated into a system of rational, intellectual reading of scripture that allowed theology and philosophy to be seen as a unity through the eyes of human intelligence. Thomas Aquinas (ca. 1225–1274), in fact, wrote tracts defending the traditional Christian theology against some Christian scholars adopting the new Islamic thought; however, Thomas did incorporate the Aristotelean philosophy and the respect for individual intellect into his own biblical studies. Thus was produced an authority for biblical study based on philosophical rational reflection that has been retained in the Catholic Church to this day.

The other innovation in biblical studies is most associated with the names of Andrew of St. Victor (died 1175) and Nicholas of Lyra (ca. 1270–340). The medieval Jewish commentators had taken up the interpretive method of Rashi such that there were dozens of Hebrew commentaries of the Hebrew Bible dealing with the literal text in Western Europe. Andrew and Nicholas studied biblical interpretation with Jewish rabbis in order to discover how Jewish tradition read Old Testament passages; it was from the rabbis that the Christian scholars received the method of historical and literal interpretation. While both scholars were well versed in Western Christian interpretation, they both introduced into their studies the grammatical and literal interpretations which they had learned from Jewish commentators. Their understanding of the literal reading of scripture became the normative method in the Western church; therefore, the "literal" reading of the Bible is not the same in the Western churches as it is among the Eastern churches.

By the time of the Council of Trent (1545–1563) the study of the literal meaning of scripture was as established as were the earlier allegorical methods. In the wake of Protestant scholarship, using only historical-literal readings of the Bible, the Bishops at Trent urged Catholic scholars to continue in the traditional exegesis of allegory. This is why allegorical interpretations continued as the most visible form of Catholic biblical scholarship into the twentieth century; however, the tradition of Andrew and Nicholas was never abandoned and has resurfaced as the dominant methodology in the Catholic Church in the late twentieth century. Officially, the Catholic Church maintains the viable authority of all traditionally approved interpretive methods for Catholic scholars of the Bible.

Protestant Churches

Those congregations in the Western church tradition that broke communion with Rome demanded that only one biblical interpretive method be used. The historical-literal reading of a text was deemed the only acceptable reading. Yet, Protestants carried much of the Roman Catholic understanding that had derived from other methods of reading the Bible into their own reading of biblical texts.

Readers

The Protestant Reformation brought many changes to the Western church where it was incorporated. Not the least of these was the insistence that the Bible should be open to all Christians for each to read individually. Wherever Protestanism was established, the Hebrew, Aramaic, and Greek texts of the Bible were translated into the vernacular of the area; the Latin Vulgate ceased to be acceptable in any Protestant tradition. The intention was that all Christians should read the Bible themselves and determine its true meaning from their own intellect. Herein the Thomist appreciation of human discernment and the literal biblical interpretation of Andrew and Nicholas combine.

In order for every Christian to read the text of the Bible and find its true and obvious meaning, Protestants insisted that there was only one level of meaning for the biblical texts. The literal reading of the Bible as history was declared the official and only acceptable interpretation for the various Protestant churches. If the Bible were properly read from a correct translation, it was believed that every Christian would come to interpret it in the same manner as all other Christians. While this notion quickly proved illusive as each Protestant group developed its own specialized "correct" literal-historical interpretation, the idea that the text clearly and literally said what any individual community said it said remains central to the Protestant churches throughout the world.

Higher Criticism and Fundamentalism

In the course of Protestant tradition, "historical-literal" interpretation has effectively divided into two general authoritative methods. One stresses the historical and the other stresses the literal. At the extreme ends of the Protestant tradition there is almost nothing in common concerning the authoritative interpretation of scripture except that the individual reader is accepted as being able to correctly understand the text.

Protestant scholars, beginning with the Reformers themselves, engaged in extensive studies of the Bible as a historical and religious document. Numerous methods were developed to aid in understanding its "original" meaning. In the process of discerning the "real" meaning of the Bible, some Protestant scholars came to regard the text and language of the Bible in the same manner they regarded any other literature, and at that point "higher criticism" was born. Higher criticism is actually a number of methods for determining the origin and meaning of biblical texts. The emphasis taken from Protestantism's "historical-critical" reading was the historical; what had actually happened in biblical times was considered of more importance than what the Bible recorded as having happened. In practice these methods deal with the Bible as a human production, eliminating divine intervention from the interpretive method.

Two seminal works created a breach within Protestantism on the use of higher-critical methods. First was David Friedrich Strauss' *Leben Jesu* (Life of Jesus) (1835–1836), a book that argued that the Gospels related myth and legend, and not much of historical value regarding the life of Jesus. Strauss lost his professorial position over this volume, but it is the basis of all subsequent searches for the "historical Jesus." Second was Julius Wellhausen's *Die Geschichte Israels* (The History of Israel) (1878), a study that worked out an evolutionary progression for the writing of the books of the Old Testament relating them to events in the history of Israel. Almost all subsequent historical reconstructions of ancient Judah and Israel and the writings deriving from them either build on this work or intentionally ignore it. For many Western Protestant denominations the various forms of higher criticism, singly or in combination, are now the authoritative methods for understanding the Bible.

Other Protestant scholars chose to emphasize the literal in the basic "historical-literal" interpretation. For these Protestants the biblical text is the absolute final authority, and higher critical methods were beyond the scope of acceptable interpretive methods. Central to this strand of Protestantism is the notion that the Bible is inerrant and has been divinely protected from human errors in transmission. A large number of evangelical scholars wrote a twelve-tract series entitled *The Fundamentals,* which was distributed beginning in ±1909 throughout Great Britain and the United States. The work set out basic assumptions and acceptable methods of Bible reading, basic to the text being the figure of Jesus as the Christ as the meaning of all biblical texts. In some ways this branch of Protestantism harks back to the Antiochene School of the early church, since it requires reading the surface literal text with an awareness of the established theology of the church (though here the theology is decidedly Western Christian). Many Protestant churches have adopted the literal method for interpretation, though the traditions for what that literal meaning is differ by denomination.

Possible Discussion Questions

1. If other religious communities base their interpretation of the Bible on a different tradition than ours, can there be common understanding of the text, or at least mutual respect for the traditions?

2. Do you understand that having an authoritative guide to interpretation (Talmud, early church authors) does not mean that all the answers to the text have been settled for all time? How might such a "lens" help or hinder Bible study?

3. Why would a religious group choose to restrict its interpretation to a literal reading, or an allegorical reading? Why do most accept both allegorical and literal meanings?

4. William Foxwell Albright attempted to straddle the "higher critical" and "fundamentalist" approaches by doing "biblical archaeology" (he was not the first, but the most famous); what problems can you imagine might develop from such an approach?

5. Reader Response Criticism claims that any text says what the reader understands it to say. Can a community be built from a Bible that can mean anything and everything that the individual members read in it?

Bibliographical Note

Aside from the general reference works, Herbert Danby, *The Misnah: Translated from the Hebrew with Introduction and Brief Explanatory Notes* (Oxford University Press, 1933); Manlio Simonetti, *Biblical Interpretation in the Early Church* (Edinburgh: T. & T. Clark, 1994); Joseph T. Lienhard, *The Bible, the Church, and Authority: The Canon of the Christian Bible in History and Theology* (Collegeville, Minn.: Liturgical, 1995); Beryl Smalley, *The Study of the Bible in the Middle Ages* (Notre Dame, Ind.: University of Notre Dame, 1964); and Emil G. Kraeling, *The Old Testament since the Reformation* (New York: Schocken Books, 1955), were consulted. Three works that can introduce the Ethiopian Orthodox biblical world to the reader: Edward Ullendorff, *Ethiopia and the Bible* (Oxford: Oxford University Press, 1968); Roger W. Cowley, *Ethiopian Biblical Interpretation: A Study in Exegetical Tradition and Hermeneutics* (Cambridge: Cambridge University Press, 1988); and Roderick Grierson, editor, *African Zion: The Sacred Art of Ethiopia* (New Haven, Conn.: Yale University Press, 1993), which has a number of Bible illustrations from Ethiopian artists.

ON TIME AND HISTORY

8

TIME AND HISTORY APPEAR TO MOST PEOPLE TO BE FAIRLY EASILY understood. Both notions, however, are complex, difficult problems and are especially so in biblical studies. How the ancient world saw time and the progression of chronological events was not exactly the same as modern scholars or church members see time. The entire notion of history and what is entailed in historical reconstruction is currently a (very heatedly) debated topic among Bible scholars. It is not the intent of this study to describe the problems of dealing with calendars in the ancient world; for those, consult a good Bible dictionary. Here, general problems with dealing in questions of time and the reconstruction of history will be presented in order that the debates in the scholarly world might be better understood and an appreciation of the problems with reading the Bible as a historical record might be grasped.

Circular and Linear

For most of the twentieth century there has been an attempt in some scholarly circles to contrast "Hebrew" notions of time with "Greek" notions of time. It has been argued, several times, that the ancient Greeks held a "circular" notion of time, whereas the ancient Israelites believed that time was "linear." The distinction is a false one, since both cultures acknowledged both cycles in history and straight, unrepeated historical movement, but the notation of the distinction has become so prevalent in biblical discussions that it needs to be addressed. Circular time refers to the recurrence of events on a regular schedule. The observance of the phases of the moon and the cycle of the sun through the year and through the constellations gave the ancient world a sense of recurring events. One could count on the seasons, the waxing and waning of the moon, and the return of star formations on a regular basis. The recording of months and weeks derived from the moon. Years could be either solar (a complete cycle of the sun through the constellations) or lunar (twelve complete cycles of the moon). The years derived from these two different observations are of different lengths (the modern Christian calendar is based on the solar year; the modern Islamic calendar is based on the lunar year—their respective months roll through each other's calendar system without exact correlation)

In the ancient world, the repetition of the years' cycles allowed for rituals to be performed to correspond to the recurring events of the seasons and months. By the time of the writing of the biblical texts, major religious centers generally used the yearly cycles to celebrate the establishment of order in their kingdoms. The beginning of the yearly cycle was often celebrated by reciting creation narratives (what we call the myths of creation) as an acknowledgment that order in a kingdom was derived from the gods by way of their chosen human representatives, the kings and queens of the various nations. This vision of the world was played out in the liturgical recreation of the world such that each year could be seen religiously as a newly created universe.

Since most deities in the ancient world had their own cult and each cult had its own cycle of ceremonies and festivals, there were numerous temporal cycles through the year, each of them repeating set religious prayers and actions in honor of their own gods. To this extent the religious world of the ancients was circular. The holy days of Judah and Israel were no different; one worshiped God on a yearly cycle, with New Year, Passover, Succoth, and all the other festivals coming around each year (and yes, it appears that creation stories were read at the Jewish New Year then as they are to this day). Whether one was Greek, Babylonian, Egyptian, Israelite, or Judean, the religious calendar was circular. It made no difference what culture you were in; the ceremonies came on a set schedule through the course of the year.

Neither Greeks nor Hebrews assumed that the events of the secular world ran in yearly cycles. In fact, no records from the ancient Near East (or anywhere else for that matter) present the notion that everything repeats itself each year. Longer cycles of recurring events, however, were believed to occur. Some Greek historians assumed that there had been cycles of civilizations that went through stages of rise and decline to be replaced, not with the same civilization, but with others that would go through the same cycle. The Bible also shows an awareness of this cyclical notion of repeated events; one need only look at the central stories of the Book of Judges with its repeated formula to see that biblical authors understood cycles in history:

> ...people forgetting God
> going after other gods
> having God send a foreign oppressor over them
> they cry out
> God hears and raises up a leader
> the leader delivers the people
> they have peace for awhile
> people forgetting God...

That is clearly cyclical history; it occurs in other biblical naratives as well. Such repeated events can be seen in another guise through the Book of Chronicles where the text presents a history with good kings and bad kings in alternating succession.

Babylonian astronomy had a notion that everything happened again exactly as it had happened before, but in cycles, called "the great year," so long that no one could possibly remember its having taken place before. The notion of millions of years worth of events being repeated was derived from determining the time it would take for all astronomical cycles to recur in exactly the same manner; a notion that was adapted by some Greek philosophers from Babylonian astronomy. That is a cyclical vision of history, but on such a grand scale that it need not concern those who are reading the Bible. The Bible itself shows no signs of understanding repeated world-ages of this type.

Linear time, on the other hand, is the acknowledgment that events happen once, that there is a past that cannot be recaptured, and a future that always stretches before one. The past cannot be changed, but the future is maleable by the actions of individuals, communities, nations, or gods in the present moment. That the Greeks produced the classic historians, all of whom were well aware that there was a past and a future and neither was going to come rolling around again, should be proof enough that the Greeks knew linear time. That individuals were born and died, that one could remember events no longer continuing, that any event that could not be replicated did not return (death of a friend, introduction of the growing of grapes, loves lost or found) gave everyone in the ancient world a notion of linear time.

The notion of a future where the events of the world converge into an end event (eschatology) is sometimes seen as a particularly linear notion of time. This is what scholars tend to refer to when they say the Hebrews had a notion of linear time. However, goals, both human and divine, for the events of this earth have a place in many ancient cultures. Possibly this idea is most notable in the Zoroastrian (religion of the Persian and, later, Parthian Empires) notion of a final judgment. Moreover, the religious traditions of Egypt, Mesopotamia, Greece, and of course Judah or Israel, knew of the far distant past and the origins of aspects of the world and of civilization. These items were established once and forever; they were not cyclical in any of these traditions.

The historical texts that form part of the Bible do not display a markedly different notion of history than do the texts of Mesopotamian historical narratives. The current biblical progression from Genesis through Kings merely tells the story of the past of the people to whom those relating the narrative belonged. The purpose of relating past events was to instruct those who heard it on how to live into the future. The combination of remembering the past and learning for the future is precisely what the Greek historians themselves claimed to be doing in their narratives about the past.

All cultures of the ancient Near East and Mediterranian knew and used both linear and circular time. Religious ritual tended to be cyclical; religious and political ambition tended to be linear. Both understandings of time need to be remembered when dealing with biblical texts.

Diachronic and Synchronic

Turning to problems of reading the Bible itself, the notions of *diachronic* or *synchronic* reading need to be understood. Both terms derive from Greek *Diachronic* means "through" (*dia*) "time" (*chronos*) and is used to refer to reading texts in a chronological order; as in, if Amos was written before Zephaniah then one needs to understand that the world had changed somewhat from the time of the former to that of the latter (if no more than to realize that the prophecies of Amos were available to the people of the time of Zephaniah, but Zephaniah's prophecies were not available to the people of the time of Amos). *Synchronic* means "with" as in "at the same" (*syn*) "time" (*chronos*) and is used to refer to reading texts that all have existence at the same time; so, for example, the Bible now forms one book; all texts that currently appear in it exist together as one volume. Since the books of the Bible now stand beside each other, any single passage in the Bible may be used to refer to all other biblical passages, regardless of when they were written or what their own history might be. So, we can read Amos having a knowledge of what appears in Zephaniah.

During the period of the composition of the various books of the Bible, the only way the authors could possibly view their work was diachronically. The authors knew that the earlier texts already existed, and they could cite them as already being authoritative. Thus, the Gospel writers make numerous references to the prophets in the Old Testament as proof texts for the activities of Jesus. The works of the Gospel writers are dependent on the prophetic literature that already had been declared sacred before they ever wrote a word. This was also true of those texts in the Old Testament that used references to earlier material in their traditions. The Book of Daniel makes reference to Jeremiah, assuming that the book of Jeremiah already existed and that it was known to the readers of Daniel.

However, once the canons have been set, the biblical books all appear together in one collection. There is, to the reader, no noticeable time difference among any of the books, since they all exist at the same moment for the one reading them. This raises the possibility of treating the Bible synchronically. All texts have equal authority, and none is seen as dependent on any other. Each passage may be read as commentary on any other. For most people in the Chrisitian tradition, this has been the manner in which the Bible has been read. Many churches continue to treat the text of the Bible as a whole, with no temporal tradition within it. Usually those reading in this manner explain that the Bible is the eternal word of God, so that, no matter when it might have been written down for human contemplation, it has existed from the creation of the world. Therefore, in this tradition, there is no real time difference related to the Bible texts. Even if one does not go so far as to assume that the Bible existed pre-creation, the reading of the text as "found text" (that is, as it currently appears on the page before the reader) is to do the same thing with the collection as to treat it as having existed from creation. This latter approach is used by literary critics whether they have any interest in the sacred nature of the Bible or not. There is a long tradition of treating the biblical texts as a unit, so that to understand the Bible as it has been read in the tradition requires one to know how one reads a text in such a manner, and it is certainly as important as knowing the historical progression of the Bible's construction and interpretation.

Keeping a Historical Perspective

Reading the Bible with a historical interest leads to at least three manners in which the text may be used. Christian and Jewish religious traditions often read the same texts and understand them differently, but, in general, there are basically three historical reconstructions with regard to the narratives found in the Bible. These range from the literal Bible text without modification to the dismissal of all narrative material in the biblical text as reflecting anything that happened in history.

Before turning to the general methods, however, "history" itself needs to be made a bit clearer. There are events that actually happen in the course of time; these events usually are simply referred to as history. However, "history" is actually a form of writing about things that happened in the past. To distinguish between the events and that which is recorded about them, let us call the events "past events." When these past events take on a special importance (say "the exodus," or "the Civil War"), one does not simply remember the past events but adds an importance to them that is held as significant by those doing the remembering; let us call these events, with their added significance, "historical events." The past events are not recoverable because there is no way to review the actual occurrences and dispassionately record everything that happened, but historical events can be debated because the meaning of past events can be changed at any time, or even have a different significance for different people (consider the American Civil War/War between the States, or the dropping of atomic bombs at the end of World War II, both of which still raise strong emotional responses among people who were not there and produce histories which view the events in diametrically opposing visions).

As for the writing of past events, the whole body of literature that deals with presenting the past in some form of chronological order is known as *historiography.* This term includes within its scope everything that purports to relate past events in any fashion. So while history appears in scholarly works as the central object of study in some sense attempting to relate past events, historiography would also include novels and historical romances that set fictional characters and situations in the context of actual past events. Historiography also includes all the socio-historical studies that attempt to demonstrate that past events fit into recurring patterns, as well as politico-historical constructs that attempt to reconstruct selected past events to further some political ambition of the writers. It does not stop there, however. Historiography also includes imaginary events that are related as if they had happened.

The notion of writing history based on an impartiality of retelling exactly what happened at some point in past events has been an ideal only since the nineteenth century and can easily be shown to be unattainable. Nonetheless, there are historians who attempt to approximate impartiality, as well as those who, knowing it is impossible, simply attempt to construe history to their liking or to bolster their own notions of the world. To someone reading modern histories, it is sometimes difficult to distinguish one approach from the other (though in some cases the difference is transparent or clearly stated by the author). In the ancient world, history was always written for some purpose beyond merely presenting past events.

In the Bible, historical events are clearly told to be of use to the readers. There is no attempt to tell everything that happened, or to refrain from having a particular viewpoint. At the very least, most of the material in the Old Testament reflects the scholarly literary circles of the Jerusalem upper classes; and the New Testament comes from a literate level of early Christians who held that there was an importance of succession of the tradition from the apostles (as opposed, say, to those who held that only the Holy Spirit should guide the church). The past, in the Bible, is edification for the future.

Bible History

Probably the vast majority of Christians read the history of the Bible from Genesis through Kings, adding Ezra, Nehemiah, First Maccabees, and then a Gospel and Acts to produce a history of the world from the biblical narratives. This method of reading history from the Bible can be called "Bible history." In the traditions of both Christianity and Judaism it has always been necessary for a scholar or religious leader to know the history as it is presented in the Bible narratives. For this historical approach, all that is needed is the text of the Bible itself. Whether the Bible presents everything that happened or even represents what actually happened in past events is unimportant. The past as presented by the Bible is all the past that the reader cares about.

This method of reading the Bible is used within the religious traditions in two manners. The more common notion is that the Bible presents exactly what happened in the past, and therefore it equates with "past events" such that no other material need be consulted in order to know the past as it was. For those who read the Bible in this fashion, proof of a past event can be demonstrated simply by citing the passage where it is reported in the Bible; no other proof can (or should) be made concerning past events. The less common use of the approach is to say that the historical progression contained in the Bible is its unique vision of the world and needs to be learned in order to understand the central teaching of the biblical texts written by those who held that vision of the past. For those in this second tradition, the correlation between past events and the biblical text may in fact be believed to be none at all, but the intention of the author to teach something of value to the readers is assumed to be recoverable by means of knowing the author's understanding of the past.

For Bible history the narratives about the past are taken to reflect the events they relate in the manner of firsthand accounts. The entirety of history from Genesis to the preaching of Paul in Rome can be accepted without questions of authorial intent or historical reconstruction on the part of the authors of the Bible. Moreover, the miraculous intervention of God and angels in the events of the world are part of the rendition of past events; to ignore the content of the texts is to ignore what happened. The document for the reconstruction of the past is taken to be authoritative for what happened, not theories about what may or may not be possible from a rationalistic point of view.

Biblical History
The second general approach to reading the biblical narratives as history relates the biblical texts to historical data from outside the Bible itself; this approach may be called "Biblical history." The

majority of European and North American biblical scholars dealing in history belong to this group, as do most European and American Christians who are interested in the Bible and its relation to history. The many books that promise to use ancient Near Eastern, Greek, or Roman texts or archaeological artifacts to support the history as presented in the Bible or to fill in gaps or background are of this type.

It is accepted by these scholars that the Bible contains material that reflects actual past events. The extent to which the Bible records accurately what happened in history is widely debated by scholars in this tradition, but all would agree that there is some historical data in the texts. Most of these scholars opt for a large amount of reliable history being retained in the Bible. While almost all of those within this group would discount miraculous intervention in the events of history, there is no consensus as to what constitutes a miracle. It is generally taken for granted that once one removes the references to angels, divine interference, and prophets reciting the word of God at opportune moments, the rest of the historical events recorded in the Bible can be taken as having happened in some manner as recorded.

Usually the earliest material in the chronology of the world is dismissed as unhistorical. So Genesis 1–11 is usually referred to as "myth" and historical studies are begun with Abraham or Moses (depending on whether or not the particular scholar believes there is evidence of Abraham, Isaac, and Jacob, or not). Some scholars begin later, believing that accurate records only exist beginning with the Judges, Saul, David, Solomon, or Rehoboam. However, it is normal among these historians to assume that the oral memory of the Judeans (often referred to as Israelites) kept earlier past events alive but perhaps in stylized fashion; so scholars debate what material may be used as serious data, which is why the starting point for solid historical reconstruction is so different for different scholars.

Since the correlation of the written biblical texts to actual past events is considered dependent on written records, the mention in the book of Kings of what appear to have been royal court records is central in the foundational theory that the histories were based on official documents. At least, it is argued, the names and succession of the rulers of Judah and Israel can be accepted as accurate, because this information would have come from those royal documents. Those stories that do not relate miraculous events can be assumed to come from archives, especially those dealing with international relations or temple matters.

Archaeological discoveries from the early nineteenth century on have been used to bolster the historical reliability of the narratives of the Bible. Cities like Nineveh and Ur were excavated, inscriptions of numerous rulers whose names appear in the Bible were unearthed, while narratives containing flood stories and primordial myths were found and deciphered. For the historians, the myths were of less importance than the hoard of material concerning Mesopotamia and Egypt that contained references to rulers known from the Bible narratives. Histories already began in the nineteenth century to combine the archaeological findings with the biblical texts to produce a "history" of the ancient world.

For New Testament scholars the method was much the same. The archaeological data came from Greek and Roman ruins, but the Bible, especially Acts, provided the model for the early history of the church. The miraculous was downplayed, and the correlations between text and known extra-biblical data became the basis for a history based on the chronology of Acts. The figure of Jesus was a more difficult problem, since no direct archaeological material related to him was (or has yet) been uncovered, but methods were worked out by which scholars assumed that they could decipher from the Gospels what was reliable tradition coming from Jesus and what was later church addition. The nineteenth-century searches for the historical Jesus continue in the flurry of books at the end of the twentieth century attempting the same kind of reconstruction.

For all of these historical reconstructions the books of the Bible are assumed to be relatively early; having been first written down within a reasonable length of time after the events recorded. For the Old Testament texts it is clear that the earliest history could not have been written by those there, but the rest of the material is given a good assessment of being accurate. While Joshua and Judges are usually seen by biblical historians to have come from the court of either David or Solomon, the scribes who recorded them are assumed to have taken the data from oral historians who had faithfully and accurately repeated the tribal histories. Samuel is assumed to come from a court narrative written by an eyewitness to the events of David's reign, while Kings currently is assumed to derive originally from the religious reforms of Josiah with some later additions. The earlier material (Genesis through Deuteronomy) is seen to contain traditions earlier than the compostion of the various sources that are presumed to range in date from David's court to the post-exilic Second Temple.

For the New Testament, the Gospels are often ascribed to the persons whose names were attached to them in the late second century, making them either eyewitnesses or second-generation witnesses. Though some scholars agree that the Gospels are all church productions by authors who had never seen Jesus, they still assume that the sayings ascribed to Jesus, at least in the Gospels of Matthew, Mark, and Luke, derive in part from an early written collection (scholars call this hypothetical collection "Q"). The Book of Acts is assumed to have been written by the end of the first century and, despite numerous literary flourishes coming from popular literature at the time (probably to increase the entertainment value of a text understood to be primarily educational in purpose), the basic story of the early church as presented in Acts is assumed to be reflective of the actual events of the early church. Correlations among the various letters in the New Testament can bolster the notion that the history of the earliest church may be approximated with the use of Acts.

In general, the scholars of this approach tend to take the Bible as trustworthy unless some narrative is shown to be false by extrabiblical evidence, or unless there is some unhistorical aspect to the narrative as the particular scholar reconstructs history; such items as flying flaming chariots or hordes of demons possessing someone often are discounted. Even so, there has been a general attempt to find a core to even ficticious narratives and miraculous events that might have been used as a historical base for the story as it now appears. The extent to which the biblical narratives may be used for reconstructing a picture of past events is highly debated among the proponents of this approach.

History of the Biblical World

The third major approach to relating the Bible and history is one used by a clear minority of modern scholars. Most of those engaged in this method of historical reconstruction are academics and not religious leaders. The notion that past events are the central concern for historians and that the Bible needs to be studied as it reflects its own historiographical representation of that world may be called "history of the biblical world." For these scholars the Bible is not a trustworthy source for reconstructing ancient past events.

Perhaps the most characteristic aspect of the scholarship of this method is the notion that the texts written for the Bible presenting its own history are compositions of a late date, with concerns for their own readers and not accurate representations of the events that they purport to relate. The Babylonian exile is usually posited as the earliest that any of the biblical books from Genesis to Kings can be dated; though currently there is a growing literature arguing that the "historical books" of the Old Testament can date no earlier than the Hellenistic Period (334–264 B.C.E.). The late dating for the writing of the biblical source texts makes the reconstruction of any past events as told in the biblical narrative suspect in the extreme as far as the scholars within this approach are concerned.

It is clear to these scholars that all of the material in the Old Testament histories has been composed to form a particular vision of the past by the authors who wrote it. Thus, Joshua or Judges cannot be taken as accurate descriptions of past events, but only as historiography by the authors of the Post-Exilic Period with a purpose to edify their own contemporaries about their own existence rather than to record actual past events. The entire literary rendition of the monarchy from Saul to Jehoiachin is taken as a morality play of sorts, such that what historical references appear in it are used to further the plot and not to hand down history as impartial data. These scholars view attempts by other historians to remove parts of biblical books to discover earlier versions (such as removing prophets from historical narratives, or stopping Kings at the reign of Josiah) as religious piety (or perhaps fraud) intent on destroying the Bible texts to further a muddled notion of the Bible as history, something they see the Bible as not. The Bible, for these scholars, is seen primarily as a theological composition and not a historical one.

Since the central concern of the scholars in this approach is to reconstruct as carefully as possible past events in a historiographical fashion, their primary interest has turned to archaeological data, extra-biblical texts, and the study of the history of the construction of the Bible (both as to its individual books and the canon). There is no need for them to turn solely to extra-biblical material to demonstrate that taking the Bible literally will not produce an accurate history of past events. One need only add up the numbers that appear in the Book of Kings for the various reigns to discover that these recorded years did not come from accurate court records (they do not add up correctly whether you attempt it with the Hebrew or the Greek texts, which use different numbers for the reigns—the numbers appear to have symbolic significance, but not "historical" accuracy). Moreover, the archaeological finds have more than sufficiently made much of the biblical narrative suspect. Attempts to reconstruct the history of Judah and Israel from archaeological data alone, of course, are impossible, since there is, despite much publicity, very little that has so far been recovered from the earth that directly relates to the events in the Bible.

New Testament scholars of similar opinions take the Gospel narratives solely as early church educational literature. For them the Greek and Roman cultural literary forms in which the narratives are written have determined the life of Jesus presented. Moreover, it is clear that the Greek form of sayings that appear in the mouth of Jesus are not the sayings that Jesus spoke in either Hebrew or Aramaic, leaving us with no words actually spoken by Jesus (at best only translations of them, but more likely early church teachings placed in Jesus' mouth). As for Acts, its use of Greco-Roman romance novel stories raises for them serious questions about the reliability of the historical basis on which it is built. Moreover, the entire Book of Acts is stylized to fit an outline and a notion of the early church as a community conforming to the Holy Spirit and the will of God, having recognized and accepted leaders. The tendency is to use the letters of Paul rather than the Book of Acts to reconstruct history; this approach provides a history which is filled with dissent and conflict, where leaders are debated and where both theology and church policy are strenuously fought over by the early Christians.

Since some (and this is not a large number) biblical texts can be shown to have historical inaccuracies in them by comparison with extra-biblical data, these scholars would prefer to have corroboration of any biblical narrative from another source before assuming it has a core in past events. The Bible is read by these scholars as religious literature with serious theological statements, but with little or no interest in reciting an accurate history of past events.

Questions for Reflection and Discussion
1. What difference does it make if one sees Hebrew (or biblical) history as linear and Greek (or secular) history as cyclical?

2. Without some biblical study, can one attempt to read the Bible diachronically? If the text is taken to be holy, what could be wrong with reading it synchronically?

3. Biblical archaeology has been very popular; what does one do with finds that clearly contradict the biblical text (some mundane examples: the reign of Sennacherib went on for decades after the point at which the Bible says he died; the city of Ai was uninhabited when Joshua says it was attacked)?

4. What are the advantages and disadvantages to each of the three manners of reading the Bible for history?

5. If history was written for directing those who read it toward the future, what does the biblical history teach us for our future?

Bibliography

A pair of books that will help introduce readers to the second and third approaches to the Bible and history in Old Testament studies: for biblical history: Baruch Halpern, *The First Historians: The Hebrew Bible and History* (San Francisco: Harper and Row, 1988); for history of the biblical world: Philip R. Davies, *In Search of 'Ancient Israel'* (2nd ed. Sheffield: Sheffield Academic Press, 1995). A survey on the different manners in which modern scholars read the same historical narratives to derive different reconstructions of past events: Lowell K. Handy, "The Reconstruction of Biblical History and Jewish-Christian Relations," *Scandinavian Journal of the Old Testament* (1991), 1: 1–22. Two very different approaches to one biblical book may be found for the Book of Acts in: Colin J. Hemer, *The Book of Acts in the Setting of Hellenistic History* (Winona Lake, Indiana: Eisenbrauns, 1990), and Richard I. Pervo, *Profit with Delight: The Literary Genre of the Acts of the Apostles* (Philadelphia: Fortress, 1987).

9   TWICE-TOLD TALES

THERE IS NOT A CANON IN THE BIBLICAL TRADITION THAT IS SO SMALL but what it contains more than one rendition of some narrative. Even the Samaritan Pentateuch includes Deuteronomy, which literally means "Second Law" and contains what is presented as Moses' recollection of the history that was just told in Exodus through Numbers. Since all biblical canons contain Deuteronomy, all Bibles include at least this duplicate narrative. The Tanak includes both Samuel and Chronicles, which provide two very different portrayals of David, one of a complex ruler gone bad and one of a good and pious king; at the same time Chronicles and Kings give us both a pious and an evil Manasseh. But it is not just individual characters who appear in multiple forms; stories about particular events come in several varieties. There are at least three creation narratives in the Bible, two renditions of the early years of the Israelites in Canaan (Joshua and Judges), and Catholics have two very different renditions of the revolt of the Hasmonaeans, not to mention the four Gospels in the New Testament. There also are duplicate renditions of some material that is not changed (Isaiah 36–39 parallels 2 Kings 18:13, 17–20:19 parallels 2 Chronicles 32:1, 9–26).

Retelling Bible Stories

Why does the Bible contain a number of different stories about the same people and events? Part of the answer, for the Old

Testament at least, can be found in the rabbinic love of debate and variation. If one reads through the Talmud it becomes clear that various positions on any topic were valued, and even theories that were rejected by most rabbis were recorded for posterity. So, in the collection of texts for the canon of the Tanak it is not strange to find contradictory opinions (Proverbs and Ecclesiastes do not agree on what wisdom is) and multiple renditions of the same history (Chronicles retells the material in Samuel and Kings, while Judges covers the same time period as Joshua).

The early church was well aware of the fact that the four Gospels that appear in the New Testament tell different stories of Jesus' life; they had the option of choosing one of those Gospels or even another for the only canonical Gospel. However, they chose to have four different Gospels, and not one consistent one, because they wanted to include the texts that were most widely used in the church and because they believed that each Gospel brought its own unique vision concerning the person and teachings of Jesus.

This is not to say that from early in both Jewish and Christian traditions there were not people who attempted to conflate all the differing narratives into one consistent story, but they appear to have been in the minority early in the tradition (however popular it became in both traditions during the Medieval Period). Most biblical scholars through the ages, however, have acknowledged the differences and have attempted to deal with them.

While there are plenty of duplicated narratives in the Catholic Bible, for example, the more books that are to be found in a given canon, the more such repeated narratives appear. What follows is a small selection of multiple renditions from various Bible canonical books and what the various renditions have done with the same material.

Creation

It is a truism of "Introduction to the Bible" courses, that the Book of Genesis begins with two, not one, creation stories. The first appears in Genesis 1:1—2:4a and the second in Genesis 2:4b—3:24. The first is called the Priestly Creation Story and portrays an all-powerful and all-knowing God who creates a "good" world through sheer command. It begins with chaos (darkness and water without form), from which an ordered world is made. The author has a very structured literary style. There is a repeated formula for each of the first six days, changed only for the particularities of each day. The first three days consist of a series of separations, and the second three days consist of populating those areas created in the first three. Thus the very orderly creation of a very competent diety looks like:

Day One:
    Separate
      Light from Darkness

Day Two:
    Separate
      Heaven from Waters

Day Three:
    Separate
      Dry land from waters
      Bonus: Vegetation

Day Four:
    Populate
      Light with lights (Sun,Moon)

Day Five:
    Populate
      Heaven with birds
      Water with fishes

Day Six:
    Populate
      Land with animals
      Bonus: Humans

Day Seven:
    Rest

Here the creation of the world is understandable and good and orderly. People (created as a group) come at the end and are very good. This is a majestic vision of God and an optimistic view of the universe.

The second creation story is called the Yahwistic Creation Narrative, and it has a different order and a different view of God, people, and the universe. It is told as straight narrative. At the beginning there is a desert without water or life. God, who is very anthropomorphic, creates mud, from which a human is fashioned. Having to sustain the human, God creates a garden in the middle of the desert. The description of the garden of Eden is filled with symbols familiar from the mythological world of Mesopotamia where they related to the homes of the gods. When the human is lonely, God creates animals; and only when all the animals have been created does God realize that only another human can be a proper partner for a human. Then God creates a second human from the first human. The rule for life in the garden for these humans is simple: do not eat fruit from the tree of knowledge of good and evil. One rule is all there is; the humans are not able to obey it. A crafty serpent (just one of the animals of the garden; the notion that this was Satan is an idea that appears long after the text was written and has nothing to do with the original Hebrew story) convinces the humans to break the one rule. For eating the forbidden fruit, the people are sentenced to lives of hardship and pain and are forced out of the garden lest they eat also from the tree of life and become gods. In this creation story, the desert without life is balanced at the end when Eve is named (mother of all living), moving from death to life. The creation was centered around the humans and yet they were not able to accept even one rule from God. The second creation story believes it is human nature to do the wrong thing. God is neither all-powerful nor all-knowing in this story but can keep people from becoming gods by keeping them from attaining immortality; it is interesting to note that the author assumes people are as knowledgeable as deities.

There is yet another creation narrative in the Old Testament. In Proverbs 8:22–31 (and in Ecclesiasticus 24, Baruch 3:9–4:4, and the Wisdom of Solomon 9–10) there is a creation story based on the construction of the world through wisdom. In this rendition, God attains wisdom as the first possession, before creation. Then God and Wisdom co-create the world in an orderly and benign fashion. The central emphasis here is that the world is a good place where people can find the proper manner of living once they grasp the order that the wisdom of God has constructed into the world. The author of the Gospel of John picks up on the wisdom creation story to produce the poem in John 1:1–18. Here Jesus has taken the place of Wisdom, but the creation of the world remains the work of the Word (=Wisdom=Jesus). All who have life receive it through the Word. For John, Jesus was pre-existent, having been from before the beginning of creation and now existing after his crucifixion.

Note that if you have the Samaritan Pentateuch as your Bible, you do not have the Proverbs Wisdom Creation story, and therefore the John poem would make no sense. Even if you can read the Proverbs passage in your canon, the connection with the John passage is not entirely clear unless you are familiar with the Wisdom Creation Narratives as they appear in Baruch and (especially) the Wisdom of Solomon. The creation narratives tell different stories; they have different purposes, but they are included in the canon because they say something of importance to those whose Bibles contain them.

Moses
The books of Exodus through Deuteronomy relate the story of Moses. However, if you happened to also have the Book of Jubilees

in your canon (Ethiopian Orthodox) then you have another vision of Moses. The central status of Moses in the Bible can be seen in every canon of the tradition. Exodus through Deuteronomy stress the leadership of Moses in bringing the people of Israel out of Egypt in the exodus, receiving the law from God on Sinai, then instructing the Israelites in its regulations, as well as being the political and military leader in the wilderness wandering. Mentioned at the end of Deuteronomy, upon the death of Moses, is that he was the greatest prophet of all time.

Jubilees picks up the notion of Moses as prophet and presents a lengthy (fifty chapters) description of what God recited to Moses while on Mount Sinai for forty days. These, the book contends, are the words of God as written down first by Moses and then by an angel for future generations. What the book contains are observations about how the Israelites will go astray once they settle in the Promised Land, lose the land, and then be restored to it. The bulk of the book, however, tells the history of the world from creation (yes, yet another different rendition of the creation) to Moses' appearance before God on Sinai to receive the law. This is a vision of Moses as author of the Torah and as a prophet who is a seer into the future, neither of which are central elements of the Exodus to Deuteronomy narratives. However, it is worth noting how the notion that Moses wrote the Torah has been common in Jewish and Christian traditions; it is a subject central to the Jubilees text, but not the Tanak.

David

The figure of King David tends to come across in Christian teaching as one of superior leadership and piety. This is the version presented in First Chronicles 10:14—29:30, where David remains a loyal ruler who reigns with justice. In the Chronicles account David's piety is demonstrated in his personally drawing up the plans for the Temple in Jerusalem, hiring all the personnel, gathering the priests and singers, and piling up the complete collection of building materials. He was not allowed to build the Temple, only because he had enlarged the kingdom through warfare, and God believed that Solomon should build the Temple in a peaceful empire. There is no conflict between Saul's house and David in Chronicles, since Saul was removed completely before David was named king. All aspects of David's political and military rule are presented in the most positive light, and the one event that is presented negatively is the census fiasco, which Chronicles insists was not David's idea or fault, and did wind up in the good result of obtaining the proper location upon which to build the Temple. For anyone who has worked his or her way through the story of David in Samuel (it starts in 1 Samuel 16) this is amazing. In Samuel the character of David is at his best an enigma and at his worst a murderous tyrant. Chosen by God as a child to replace Saul as king of Israel, David comes to the king's court by one of four narratives where he becomes good friends with Jonathan, Saul's heir apparent. David quickly assumes the position of heir apparent by having Jonathan turn the office over to him. Saul, supposedly crazy, seeks David's life, so David flees to the area of Judah, where he sets up a protection racket, demanding payments to protect caravans moving through the area. He also picks up beautiful women, a failing that returns to doom him. With Saul attempting to run him down, David eventually signs up as a mercenary soldier in the employ of the Philistines (Israel's most dangerous enemies). When Saul is slain in battle with the Philistines, David becomes king of Judah, then of Israel (through some double crosses and treason, but not by David himself). All goes well with David until he takes the wife of one of his generals and has the general slain. For this his house is condemned to eternal turmoil. His son and heir apparent, Amnon, rapes his daughter, Tamar, leading to Absalom's slaying his half-brother Amnon, and eventually to the first of three revolutions by the populace against David. By the end of Samuel, God still likes David, but the population hates him; he stays in power solely because of his own private mercenary army.

Both Jewish and Christian literatures present David as the figure to model the ruler upon. The whole notion of the coming Messiah, whether by the Jews who became Christians or of the Jews who await the coming of the Messiah, is based on a just and pious David figure. So, while the narrative found in Chronicles is decidedly the less well-known of the two accounts, the religious traditions know David only through the Chronicles account and often reinterpret the Samuel account to force it to fit the "nicer" version.

Ezra

Ezra may not spring to mind among Christians as one of the most important figures in the Bible, but he is. By tradition, Ezra compiled the Torah and presented it to Judah after the exile in Babylonia. This explains why there are a total of four books named after him that appear in assorted Christian canons. Depending on which of the books you pick up in "your" canon, Ezra is merely a Persian functionary, the singlehanded restorer of Judah after the exile, or a prophet.

The large scroll "Ezra," which now appears as the two books Ezra and Nehemiah, relates the history of the Israelites as they returned to their homeland and set about rebuilding their Temple. Ezra appears here as the Jewish scribe serving as a Persian bureaucrat who accepts the commission to compile Jewish law and then proclaim it in Judea, part of the Persian Empire. Nehemiah comes and enforces these rules. All this is told from documents supposed to derive from the files of Ezra and Nehemiah themselves.

First Esdras, as named in the Protestant tradition (Third Esdras in traditional Roman Catholic Bible's apocryphas, Second Esdras in the Russian Orthodox Bible), is a variant spelling of Ezra. This short book presents a short history of the need for and mission of Ezra after the exile. Beginning with the cult reform of Josiah, the story of the exile and the commissioning of Ezra, as well as his proclamation of the Torah to the Jews, is told in a parallel format to the material appearing in Chronicles and Ezra and Nehemiah. One major difference, however, is that the role of Nehemiah is reduced to almost nothing, so that Ezra becomes the single major rebuilder of Judea.

Second Esdras, as named in the Protestant tradition (Fourth Esdras in Roman Catholic Bible's apocryphas, Third Esdras in the Russian Orthodox Bible), is the book of Ezra that presents him as a prophet. Here Ezra has a call to prophetic ministry, as had Isaiah and Ezekiel. The work consists of seven visions seen by Ezra and explains the division between Israelites and those who are true followers of God. In the course of explaining his visions to Ezra, God states that some things are beyond human understanding, yet God's grace overcomes the sin of individuals when they believe in God and join in the cosmic battle against evil. Just to keep things confusing, there are two versions of Fourth Esdras, an "Eastern" and a "Western," the latter having a preface and conclusion containing visions of the end battle between the heavenly victors and the hellish losers in the final confrontation between good and evil.

Those Hasmonaeans

Aside from the Protestant Bible, most Christian Bibles contain the first two books named Maccabees. Both of these works describe the revolt of the pious Jews against Antiochus IV, King of the Seleucids, when he decided to outlaw Judaism in his empire. However, one book (1 Maccabees) sees the leading family of the revolt, the Hasmonaeans, in a highly favorable light and the other (2 Maccabees) sees them as evil. The name "Maccabees" comes from the nickname of Judas, one of the sons, which means "hammerer"; it came to be associated with the entire dynasty only after the dynasty ceased to exist.

First Maccabees presented a Hebrew history based on the writing style of the Former Prophets. In this version the heroes of the story were all the members of the Hasmonaean family, beginning with the father, Matthias, who discovered that to save the Torah from being destroyed, he would have to break the rules in it (if your army cannot fight every seventh day, it does not take the enemy long to figure out how to beat you soundly). The villains include all Gentiles (except Romans and Spartans), but especially Antiochus IV, who set out to convert or destroy the Jews. In this history, events are presented as occurring in an essentially natural fashion, with the best death one can hope for being to die in glorious battle defending the Hasmonaean dynasty, which had been set up after they defeated the Seleucid kings. To a large extent the book was written to explain why the Hasmonaeans should be treated as the new Davidic dynasty.

Second Maccabees tells the same history, but in a totally different way. To begin with, it was a Greek history (condensed from five volumes written by Jason of Cyrene); it only finds one Hasmonaean, Judas, acceptable, because he restored the Temple. The real heroes of the book are those Jews who kept all the laws of the Torah no matter what the consequences, especially the High Priest Onias III. The real villains of the story are those Jews who broke any of the laws of the Torah and two high priests of the Temple who bought their positions, Simon and Menelaus (Antiochus IV comes across in Second Maccabees more as misinformed than as evil). Since the Hasmonaean Simon became both king and priest in violation of Torah law, Second Maccabees calls upon all true Jews to reject the Hasmonaeans as rulers. The story is told with miracles, prophetic announcements, and divine intervention. The best death is presented as the possibility that one might die in martyrdom keeping the Torah. The book is the first place where notions of either "creation from nothing at all" or resurrection of the righteous appear in the Jewish tradition.

If two histories with polar opposite views of the central figures are not confusing enough, there are two more books called Maccabees that appear in various Christian Old Testament canons. Third Maccabees is not about the Hasmonaeans at all, but a (rather wild) story about persecution in Ptolemaic Egypt. In Fourth Maccabees the history of the first two books appears only as a backdrop to a philosophical treatise on the relation between reason and passion.

Jesus: Infancy Narratives

Every Christmas millions of creches come out of boxes and are set up throughout the world; they have sheep and camels, shepherds and wise men, angels and a manger. Matthew tells a story of Jesus' birth, and Luke tells a story of Jesus' birth. They are not the same story. However, Christmas tradition has combined them. Both Gospels relate a variation on two different standard stories found in the ancient world for the births of famous people. Those stories and their basic forms are:

THE HERO EXPOSED AT BIRTH	THE HERO FORETOLD
1. Child has to be abandoned	1. Birth foretold by divine agent
2. Child of noble birth	2. Birth a physical impossibility
3. Agent saves child from certain death	3. A divine presence at conception
4. Future child dedicated before birth	4. Child exposed
5. Child named at birth	5. Nursed/raised by humans
6. Adopted by royalty/ cleric/deity	6. Hero becomes what dedicated to be
7. Stories of great deeds	

The Gospel of Matthew used the "Hero Exposed" narrative (which can also be found used in the Bible for Moses, Exodus 2:1–10, and Joash, 2 Kings 11:1–3) while the Gospel of Luke used the "Hero Foretold" story (which can also be found in the Bible used for Isaac, Genesis 17:15–19; 18:9–15; 21:1–7, Samson, Judges 13:1–25, and Samuel, 1 Samuel 1:1–2:11).

Matthew's infancy narrative presumes that Mary and Joseph lived in Bethlehem, were visited by priests from Parthia, had to flee to Egypt from the certain death decreed by King Herod, and only went to Nazareth after the king's death because it was dangerous to return to their hometown. The characters here are important and rich; a wealth that is turned over to the baby Jesus. The angel appears to Joseph, whereas Mary plays a minor role in the story.

Luke centers on Mary; Joseph plays the minor role. Both John the Baptist and Jesus are given variations of the same stock birth narrative. It is clear that the story of Samuel's birth is the pattern for Luke's rendition, complete with songs. Here Mary and Joseph have had to travel from Nazareth, their homeland, to fill out forms for taxes for Rome. Poverty and homelessness emphasize their powerlessness. The angels talk to Mary and sing to shepherds (the bottom of the social ladder in the ancient world). The couple waits eight days and then goes to the Temple in Jerusalem and on home to Nazareth. The promise of God to raise up the poor (a central theme in the Gospel of Luke) is emphasized already in the infancy story.

Just to keep things interesting, John also presents a sort of infancy narrative in the opening poem. Taking the Wisdom Creation Story, the author declares that the Wisdom(=Word) who created the world became incarnate in the world (1:14) in order to bring the light (wisdom) of God to the world that knows it not. Since wisdom was seen in the earlier literature as bringing life, this wisdom is portrayed bringing eternal life. This incarnation narrative, like those in Matthew and Luke, is using an earlier Jewish theological literary tradition to express the birth of Jesus; here a pre-existent being who became human and then returned to heaven.

Jesus: Resurrection Narratives
Each Gospel has its own resurrection narrative. They are not the same story. Mark, the earliest written Gospel, originally had no resurrection story at all. Now it has different endings in different Bibles. The women fled from the empty tomb and told no one at the ending of the original text (Mark 16:8). As the work was copied, the copiers added resurrections to have the work conform to other gospels with which they were familiar.

Matthew, who had stressed the teachings of Jesus and the slow but certain learning process of the disciples, ends with the "Great Commission" to his disciples, which assumes that they are capable of teaching what they were taught. This takes place in Galilee on a mountain. The high place is significant, since Matthew uses the symbolism of the mountain as a place where one encounters God; remember, this is the Gospel of the Sermon of the Mount.

Luke stressed eating as a symbolic act that bore meaning and understanding. The disciples in Luke had known, if not perfectly, who Jesus was from the beginning of their study with

Jesus; so the Gospel resurrection narrative begins not with the disciples, but with two followers of Jesus not of the innermost circle. They meet Jesus on the road leading out of Jerusalem and only recognize him in the breaking of bread. When Jesus appears to the disciples, they are in Jerusalem and are amazed, but he stays for forty days to teach them everything they need to know before he ascends into heaven.

John has Jesus appear to Mary Magdelene in the garden when she finds the tomb empty. The disciples first meet him while locked in a room in Jerusalem. Thomas is absent and doubts both the other disciples and then Jesus himself. They are told that they are the first of a series of witnesses to the truth, a theme that has run through the Gospel from the very first notice given to John the Baptist. This is followed by another appearance by the sea where the disciples have (suprisingly) returned to their former work. Jesus assigns Peter his place as the head of the disciples and tells him he will be crucified.

Very different stories, but each suited to the individual Gospel narrative. The later church attempted to conflate the different narratives to the same result as the infancy narratives; all the resurrection stories are often told as one series of events. In fact, each emphasizes the central aspects of their own rendition of the life and teachings of Jesus.

Questions for Reflection and Discussion

1. The church traditionally has smoothed over the different renditions of the same story or character. Is there some way that the different renditions would be useful for the teaching of the church?

2. With so many Creation stories in the Christian canons (don't forget Jubilees), what does this suggest about the telling of world formation in the tradition?

3. It has been noticed that there was a tendancy in the period of the early church to read famous people of the past as prophets and then to write out the texts for these persons; we mentioned Moses and Ezra, but there were many others (including Enoch). Why might this understanding of these people from earlier times have developed?

4. Why would one use a stock story to write about a famous person's birth?

5. Can you think of other stories or characters that have duplicate narratives within your canon (or in other canons of the tradition)?

Bibliographical Note

Some of these repeated narratives have been studied in detail, but mostly (as here) a simple reading of the texts suffices to tell the difference; the "Hero Exposed at Birth" outline has been adapted from Brian Lewis, *The Sargon Legend: A Study of the Akkadian Text and the Tale of the Hero Who Was Exposed at Birth*, Dissertation Series 4 (Cambridge: American Schools of Oriental Research, 1980). Following are a few books that might be helpful: Claus Westermann, *Creation*, translated by John J. Scullion (Philadelphia: 1971); Jonathan A. Goldstein, *I Maccabees*, Anchor Bible, 41 (Garden City, N.Y.: Doubleday, 1976), and *II Maccabees*, Anchor Bible, 41A (Garden City, N.Y.: Doubleday, 1983); Raymond E. Brown, *The Birth of the Messiah: A Commentary of the Infancy Narratives in Matthew and Luke*, 2nd edition (New York: Doubleday, 1993); and by the same author, *The Death of the Messiah: From Gethsemane to the Grave: A Commentary on the Passion Narrative of the Four Gospels,* 2 volumes (Garden City, N.Y.: Doubleday, 1994); as well as Norman Perrin, *The Resurrection According to Matthew, Mark, and Luke* (Philadelphia: Fortress, 1977). Even small sayings of Jesus can be given different interpretations in the various New Testament renditions; a good example can be found in Mary W. Patrick, *The Love Commandment: How to Find Its Meaning for Today* (St. Louis, Mo.: Chalice Press, 1984).

AND LITURGY

IN LUKE 4:15–27, THERE IS AS EARLY A DESCRIPTION OF A SYNAGOGUE service as exists. The center of the service was the reading and expounding of a biblical text. In Jewish and Christian worship services to this day, wherever they are held throughout the world, the center of the service remains the reading and interpretion of the Bible.

The Origins of the Liturgy

The beginnings of Jewish and Christian worship services can be found in the Temple services in Jerusalem; unfortunately, the record of worship services for the First Temple (the one destroyed in 586 B.C.E. by the Babylonians) no longer exists, nor can it be reconstructed from existing sources. On the other hand, the Mishnah and Gemara include numerous recollections of the services of the Second Temple (the one destroyed in 70 C.E. by the Romans). By the time of the Roman destruction of the Temple, reading biblical passages and reciting or singing particular psalms were part of the regular Temple ritual. With the Temple's destruction, the center of Jewish worship necessarily defaulted to the weekly Sabbath synagogue services.

The synagogue service was the foundation upon which all Jewish and Christian worship liturgies was based. Its origins are unknown. By tradition, Ezekiel introduced synagogue services for the Judeans exiled in Babylonia in the sixth century B.C.E. when they could not attend the rituals of the Temple in Jerusalem or even mark the time when those services were held, since the Babylonians had destroyed the Temple itself. By the time evidence does exist for synagogue services, in the passage in Luke and in the Mishnaic teachings about proper texts and prayers, the institution had already been long established.

Jewish Liturgy

The central event of the Sabbath service was the reading of the Torah. In a three-year (one-year if in Mesopotamia) period the Torah was (and is) to be recited in its entirety. Prophetic passages (called haftarah) came to be read and discussed on certain Sabbaths of the year as a secondary reading to the Torah, but, unlike the Torah, the haftarah readings are not in biblical textual order. Exactly when definitive biblical passages were introduced into the service to form a lectionary is unknown; however, the early church adopted this practice, so it clearly was already in use in the early centuries C.E. Reading the Torah was required, the prophets were popular, and the writings (with the exception of the psalms that were a constituent part of the service) were scattered around the year.

In Palestine it was the custom for one of the members of the congregation to be asked to read from the scrolls. It was expected in the first century C.E. that adult male Jews would have been trained in Hebrew, but in reality, the reading would have necessarily been restricted to those who had sufficient education to be able to read a language that had ceased to be spoken in the daily lives of most of the Jewish population. In Mesopotamia, each synagogue had a member whose duty it was to read the Bible passages for the services; the other members were not required to read. The text was read from scrolls kept in the ark (a cabinet located at the front of the worship area). It was not the custom to translate the sacred text from the original language; scripture was read in Hebrew, then discussed in the vernacular of the area in which the synagogue was located. Learned rabbis could make extended speeches on the interpretation of the passages of the morning, originating the "homily."

Until the seventeenth century it was the custom to preface Friday evening Sabbath services by reciting the Song of Solomon; it was believed that the allegorical interpretation of the lovers in the book referred to God and the Sabbath Day. In the seventeenth century it became normal in Eastern Europe to recite Psalms 29 and 95–99. The service itself traditionally begins with the communal recitation of the *shema* (Deuteronomy 6:4–9) and ends with a hymn. The Sabbath morning service begins with a series of psalms and the *shema*. The liturgical readings for the Torah are recited along with the appropriate haftarah for the Torah passage. In modern times there usually is a meditation on the passages of the morning by the rabbi, and the services end with the recitation of Psalm 145 and a hymn.

Those who read and those who heard the text originally took part in a discussion of the meaning of the passages of the day. Both what the text meant of itself and what use might be made of it for their daily lives were open for discussion. In the coming together of the Jewish population as a community to hear and interpret the Bible, Jewish identity was maintained in the far reaches of the Jewish diaspora ("Jewish diaspora" refers to all areas where Jews settled outside of the land that had been Judah and Israel). In the repeating of the Torah and the reflection upon what it meant to be part of a religious people, the synagogue services provided social coherence and social instruction, as well as spiritual guidance.

The holy days of the Jewish year, which themselves are derived from the Torah, call for special readings from the Bible. Usually the passages that describe the foundation of the day as holy are read, as well as texts that are related to the main themes of the day, either literally or allegorically. The "five scrolls" are read in their entirety during their respective proper celebrations: Song of Songs at Passover (symbolizing the love of God for Israel), Ruth at the Feast of Weeks (celebrating the reception of the Law from God, the story is understood to represent that the Law goes out to whoever wishes to live under it), Lamentations at the Ninth of Ab (fast commemorating the destruction of the Temple), Ecclesiastes at Sukkot (booths to prepare for the coming winter), and Esther at Purim (celebrated as a sort of carnival in remembrance of the escape from Haman's evil plan).

Early Synagogue and Early Church

All first-generation Christians were Jews. It was the custom of the early church members to attend synagogue services on Sabbath as they always had. They distinguished themselves from the other members of the synagogues to which they belonged by also meeting on the day after Sabbath, which they came to call "Lord's Day," since it was on Sunday that Jesus was understood to have arisen. The worship service of the synagogue was used as the basis for the Lord's Day service as well. The early Christians sang hymns, prayed, and, of course, read scripture. The scripture they used was the Torah and the Prophets (with whatever Writings their local synagogue had accepted, but always the Psalms); these they studied in light of their new understanding of Jesus as the risen Messiah. Suddenly, the old texts had new and totally different meanings for them. In their own services the Bible was read in light of interpretations relating to Jesus as the Messiah.

It is clear from references made in the Gospels that numerous passages from the prophetic books of the canon were immediately understood by the first Christians as referring to Jesus. Perhaps the most influential passages were those of the Suffering Servant poems of Isaiah (Isaiah 42:1–9; 49:1–13; 50:4–11; 52:13–53:12) since they clearly form the underlying theological structure to the Passion Narrative that is found in all four canonical Gospels. However, it was not only prophetic texts that were incorporated into early church use; the Psalms had been central in Temple and synagogue services, and they were taken over into early Christian worship as songs about Jesus as Messiah (note the centrality of Psalm 110 in Hebrews). If the center of the synagogue service had been the Torah, it also could be read with Christian eyes. Moses was seen as a "type" for Jesus as Savior, the flood as a "type" for Jesus' death and resurrection, or the wilderness wandering after the exodus as the dangers of Christian backsliding. The opening poem in John takes one strand of theology concerning the Torah (and wisdom personified) as existing from before creation (see the Book of Baruch or the Wisdom of Solomon) and reads it as a description of Jesus as the pre-existent Messiah; whereas the Torah itself had been the center of the Jewish service, for the church it was replaced with discussion of Jesus as the risen Christ.

It was the custom in the early church to center the services on the memory of Jesus' last meal. The Lord's supper developed into the liturgical eucharist, or mass, based on the words recorded as having been spoken by Jesus to his disciples as appearing in Matthew, Mark, and Luke in their Passion Narratives where the Jewish Passover seder was reinterpreted by Jesus for his disciples. In Orthodox and Catholic eucharistic liturgies almost the entire service is based on biblical texts. The passages of the Sunday services early in the church consisted of the chanting of a psalm (taken directly from the synagogue service), the reading of a biblical passage (though Christians tended toward the Prophets, as foretelling Christ, rather than the Torah), and the discussion of the passage read that day, which quickly became a "homily," that is, a "sermon" by a leader in the congregation. To these parts of the service (all taken from the synagogue) were added readings from works created by the church itself. Letters from church leaders were read to the congregations, and the story of the life of Jesus became part of the normal Sunday service as well. This developed long before there was an accepted New Testament; the Bible was still "the Law and the Prophets." Once a New Testament was designated, it became standard to have four sets of passages read in each worship service: an Old Testament reading (any passage from the accepted canon of the Old Testament), a Gospel reading (from Matthew, Mark, Luke, or John), an Epistle reading (originally from one of the letters in the New Testament, now it means any New Testament passage not a Gospel), and a Psalm (one or more of the poems from the Book of Psalms). These four designations of the biblical texts remain standard throughout the overwhelming majority of Christian congregations.

The Christian Liturgical Year: Orthodox Church

Modern churches base their worship services on a liturgical calendar that completes a cycle each solar year. Most denominations begin their years with Advent, leading up to the celebration of Christmas; however, the earliest church did not celebrate Christmas at all, and the entire liturgical year centered on the Easter service. In Orthodox liturgy, where the celebration of the church service retains its central importance from the first centuries of Christianity, the heart of the Christian year is "Great Lent," the period of preparation for Easter. The extensive liturgy for Great Lent is contained in the service manual the *Triodion.* A brief survey of this season will demonstrate the centrality of scripture in the Orthodox services.

Lent itself is a forty-day period of self-reflection and fasting that prepares the Christian for celebrating the resurrection of Jesus as the Christ. In Orthodox liturgy there are four Sunday services that lead up to Lent itself; each is based on a biblical passage and deals with an aspect of preparation on the part of the individual for the lenten season ahead. The Sunday of Zacchaeus (Luke 19:1–10) reflects on the desire of the believer to see Jesus; the sermon reflects on the anticipation of and the worthiness of the congregation for the coming of

Easter. The Sunday of the Publican and the Pharisee (Luke 18:10–14] begins a series of sermons on repentance; this first service stresses the need for true humility and a serious self-evaluation before God. The Sunday of the Prodigal Son (Luke 15:11–32) continues the repentance theme by illustrating the return of the sinner to the love of God, while acknowledging the exile in which the individual believers now find themselves. The Sunday of the Last Judgment (Matthew 25:31–46) stresses the mercy of God for those who repent. The Sunday of Forgiveness (Matthew 6:14–21) reflects upon the exile of Adam from Eden and on the need of forgiveness not only from God, but also from each Christian for all others.

For the season of Lent itself, the Orthodox Church holds an "incomplete" eucharistic service each day, with special services on Wednesday, Friday, and Saturday, and each Sunday service emphasizes an aspect of the church tradition or an appropriate saint. In the sixth week of Lent and during the entirety of Holy Week, the services relate the continuous narrative of the Passion. The penitence of Lent officially ends with two days of joy, beginning with the Saturday of Lazarus and ending with Palm Sunday, which begins Holy Week. Holy Week itself is prefaced with the Saturday of Lazarus, when the faithful rejoice at Christ's victory over death on behalf of a friend (John 11:1–46); the service stresses Christ's two natures: divine and human. Palm Sunday relates the story of Jesus' triumphal entry into Jerusalem and is known as the Sunday of Christ the King. Palm branches are blessed and held, along with lighted candles, by the congregation through the service. The great joy of Palm Sunday is followed by three days of sombre reflection.

Monday through Wednesday of Holy Week is given over to contemplation of the teachings of Jesus in the last days of his life. Monday is dedicated to the memory of Joseph (son of Jacob), who was falsely punished, as a symbol both of the crucifixion of Jesus and the fate of the unrepentant. Tuesday remembers the Ten Virgins of Matthew's parable (Matthew 25:1–3), showing those who waited patiently for or did not prepare well for the coming of the Lord. Wednesday is dedicated to the memory of the woman who anointed Jesus' feet with her hair (Matthew 26:6–13 and Luke 7:36–50) and who received forgiveness even though a sinner, unlike Judas, who did not understand and delivered Christ to death. Holy Thursday (Maundy Thursday) celebrates four events in the Passion: the ritual of washing feet, the institution of the eucharist, the agony of Gethsemane, and the betrayal by Judas; all are biblical events.

Good Friday is known as "Great Friday" in Orthodox services. The service for Great Friday begins the evening before with the reading of twelve Gospel passages that relate the story of Jesus' Passion, beginning with the speech at the Last Supper and ending with the burial. At the sixth reading, the presence of Christ's death among the congregation is understood; Greek Orthodox services usually symbolize this by moving the sanctuary crucifix from its accustomed place to the center of the congregation. Great Friday itself is a day of great sorrow; there is no eucharist of any kind celebrated. Each hour a lectionary reading of an Old Testament, an Epistle, and a Gospel passage is solemnly recited. The death, burial, and lamentation for Christ is read and enacted. Passages from the crucifixion scenes of the four Gospels and lines from the Book of Lamentations and the lament psalms form major portions of the day's readings. Friday evening begins the Holy Saturday observance by preparing for the Easter Vigil; the burial of Christ and the descent into hell are remembered and the congregation begins waiting with expectation, ending the service itself with the rituals of a funeral service.

Holy Saturday services follow traditional liturgies worked out through the centuries, but in the evening the all-night Easter Vigil takes place. In the early church, baptisms were regularly held during the course of the vigil as Holy Saturday passed into Easter morning. For this reason a number of passages read during Easter Vigil reflect the typological understanding of Old Testament passages. The first creation story of Genesis, the flood, the passing of the Israelites through the Red Sea are all read as reflections of baptism; in addition, Passover texts are read to remember God's saving grace, and resurrection typological texts are presented. By midnight all lights in the church are extinguished and all sounds cease until, at midnight, a priest comes forth with a single candle representing the light of the risen Christ (a symbolism derived from the Gospel of John). Easter has come.

Easter season lasts to Pentecost. Pentecost was a Jewish holy day fifty days after Passover; the church celebrates it as the coming of the Holy Spirit. The church calendar from Pentecost until Advent is known as "Trinity," "Ordinary Time," or just "Pentecost Season" and traditionally has been a period of Bible readings with little or no correlation to each other. With four Sundays that make up Advent, the church looks forward to Christmas, so the biblical passages tend toward prophetic passages in the Old

Testament readings that have come to be understood as predicting Jesus, whereas the New Testament Gospel passages relate the texts prior to the Infancy Narratives of Jesus. It was believed that the magi came to see Jesus twelve days after his birth, and so Epiphany appears twelve days after Christmas, forming the twelve-day Christmas season in the Western church; in many of the Eastern churches, Epiphany is Christmas. Epiphany season extends to Lent and usually is devoted to the celebration of the life of the humanly Jesus among humans. In this way the life of Jesus is summed up each year from Advent to Easter.

Liturgical Readings

Passages read for the church service each Sunday are usually not of the choosing of the pastor, priest, or minister. Many Protestant churches do pick one or two Bible verses to suit the sermon of the morning, simply by seeking out the passages that the minister wishes to speak on (or around). In most churches the Bible passages are taken from a *lectionary*. A lectionary is an official calendar of biblical verses selected by a denomination to be read in the service for each day of the week, but especially for the Sunday and Holy Day services. By using a set series of biblical texts, all churches within a denomination are focusing on the same passages of scripture on any given Sunday. The most widely used lectionary is, of course, that of the Roman Catholic Church; however, a number of Protestant denominations have agreed on a common selection of passages that is called "The Common Lectionary" and is shared by Protestant congregations ranging from Lutheran and Presbyterian to the United Church of Christ and the Christian Church (Disciples of Christ). The Orthodox churches have their own lectionaries, often devised by outstanding liturgists in the individual traditions of the various Orthodox communities.

The current lectionaries used by churches in the West derive from a decision made by the Roman Catholic bishops who met at the Second Vatican Council (1962–1965). It was decided that it would be good for the church to cover a particular Gospel in a year rather than to jump around in the readings from Gospel to Gospel each Sunday. Three-year cycles of lectionary readings allow the church to cover each of the Synoptic Gospels ("synoptic" means they look alike; it refers to Matthew, Mark, and Luke, all of whom use similar stories and parables, and present a similar vision of Jesus) in a fairly complete manner. The Gospel of John appears at various times throughout the three year cycle, but every year is used on certain Sundays in Advent, Lent, and Easter. This also allows "Ordinary Time" to be used for a coherent series of sermons rather than the unorganized selections of passages previously chosen for the lectionary readings.

The traditional set of readings for a particular service were to be retained. Therefore, a complete lectionary reading for any given day contains an Old Testament passage, a Gospel passage, an Epistle passage, and the Psalm of the day. In the new system it would be the Gospel passage that would determine the other passages, all readings to be related to each other and suitable for incorporating into the sermon. In most churches the Gospel passage is read, while often either the Epistle or Old Testament reading is left unread. The Psalm passage is often ignored in Protestant lectionary usage, though many churches incorporate it into the service by means of a cantor or by public singing (many popular church hymns derive from the Geneva Psalter, an attempt by the early Reformed churches to incorporate the psalm readings of the Roman Catholic lectionaries of the sixteenth century into the Protestant services by having the congregation sing them). Some congregations merely pick one of the four readings given for a day and use it as the sole passage.

Since the traditions surrounding Advent, Christmas, Holy Week, and Easter have become so established, it was determined that traditional readings for these seasons would be retained in the new lectionaries. This means not only that a variety of Gospels appear in succeeding Sundays, but that passages selected originally for typological or allegorical reasons remain in the lectionaries. However, after Pentecost, there is sufficient time to seriously investigate each of the Synoptic Gospels. In Year A of the lectionary the passages come primarily from Matthew, in Year B from Mark, and in Year C from Luke. The rule of thumb for determining which year one is in is to remember that any year that can be evenly divided by three is "Year C" and devoted to the Gospel of Luke.

Some Liturgical Reading Problems

Not all biblical passages are readily adaptable to church use, so some sections of the Bible are not regular liturgical readings. Though Nahum, Obadiah, Song of Songs, Third John, and Jude all appear in the canon, the Christian church does not make much use of any of them in the lectionary. Nahum and Obadiah may appear when a congregation is feeling particulary militant, but for a regular cycle of readings the condemnation of enemies to death and destruction with a sense of unbridled glee has been understood generally to be inappropriate. The Song of Songs, previously so popular as allegory in the church, has suffered the fate of having become literal in the past century; many church liturgies tend to avoid passages that are highly sexually erotic as texts of the morning. Third John is a cover letter for First John, and it is hard to use an introduction to a letter carrier with a few nasty side comments as the basis of an edifying sermon. Jude has the problem of accepting as canonical texts two works that are not considered canonical by most churches (The Assumption of Moses is accepted by no churches and Enoch only by the Ethiopian Orthodox). The great legal corpus of Exodus, Leviticus, and Deuteronomy, though central to the Jewish Torah cycle, tends to be ignored by most Protestants, though Reformed churches, after the model of John Calvin, do make use of them positively; and Lutheran churches, after the model of Martin Luther, tend to bring them in only as "law," to which the "gospel" may be contrasted. Needless to say, the first nine chapters of First Chronicles are not favorite lectionary readings in any tradition.

Almost no passage read in a congregation treats the Bible text by itself. Christians have tended from the beginning to read their Bible through the lens of the New Testament texts. The legal material of the Torah becomes a very different body of literature if Paul is one's guide. The meaning of any given biblical passage changes when considered in light of other passages on the same topic or with a different concept. The books that actually appear in a congregation's canon, therefore, determine what various passages actually mean. Protestant lectionaries do not contain the apocryphal books that appear in Catholic lectionaries (an exception occurs in Anglican and Lutheran lectionary readings for All Souls and All Saints Days, where Ecclesiasticus 44:1 and following is often the Old Testament passage of the day). However, the differences in canons is one major explanation of why all churches do not use the same lectionary.

The translation of the Bible in use in a given service has been an interesting problem. Until the Second Vatican Council, the Catholic Church read from the Vulgate, despite Latin having ceased to be a spoken language anywhere on earth (aside from the Vatican itself). The Russian Orthodox Church still uses Old Slavonic for Bible readings and the liturgy, despite its never having been understandable to the congregation. Many Protestants continue to use the King James Version, despite its archaic language and occasional mistranslations (remember those unicorns). New translations attempt to put understandable words in the hearing of the community. In an attempt to make the word as accessible as possible, modern church lectionary readings have adopted such lectionary adaptations as vernacular language (what the actual people of the congregation use and understand themselves), gender inclusive language (translations of texts that reflect the non-gender, non–sex-oriented intentions of the Bible or its translators), and cultural exclusion (selecting texts that cannot be mistaken in the modern world for evil purposes that the church does not intend, as well as not using passages that can be misconstrued [or even correctly construed, but cannot any longer be tolerated as Christian teaching]). Any such attempts to introduce Bible readings that are not familiar tend to be met with opposition by congregations; however, the effort is to make the liturgy as relevant as possible and still get the Christian message across.

Since the words of liturgy carry so much meaning, it is necessary to use them with care. The heart and soul of the liturgical service is the Bible and the narratives the Bible relates. Therefore, the words read as the canonical Bible are of central importance, and much thought needs to be expended on exactly what one means to have the congregation hear when the word (or the Word) is spoken. For this, the meaning of the word not only for the reader, but also for the audience needs to be considered. It is not enough that the word of God be spoken; the word of God needs to be heard.

Questions for Reflection and Discussion

1. What ties Jewish, Orthodox, Catholic, and Protestant Bible readings in worship together?

2. What are the possible advantages of having all four liturgical readings (Old Testament, Gospel, Epistle, Psalm) for one service?

3. Does your congregation use a lectionary? Get a copy and see how it arranges readings for Sunday services and for holidays.

4. What kind of Bible should be used for scripture readings? How should it be adapted for your congregation? Would you prefer having the texts read in the Hebrew or Greek?

5. Protestants say expounding the Word is the center of their worship service; Orthodox liturgists say the Word is the center of

liturgy in both word and action in the Eucharist. What difference is there in having the Bible seen as central in liturgical presentation or in lectionary readings?

Bibliographical Note

The following books were useful in preparing this chapter or may be useful for those interested in investigating questions of liturgy. On the early liturgy: *The Jewish Roots of Christian Liturgy*, edited by Eugene J. Fisher (New York: Paulist, 1990), and Josef A. Jungmann, *The Early Liturgy: To the Time of Gregory the Great*, Liturgical Studies, 6 (Notre Dame, Ind.: University of Notre Dame, 1959). On Jewish liturgy: A. Z. Idelsohn, *Jewish Liturgy and Its Development* (New York: Schocken Books, 1960), Abraham P. Bloch, *The Biblical and Historical Background of the Jewish Holy Days* (New York: KTAV, 1978), and Ismar Elbogen, *Jewish Liturgy: A Comprehensive History*, translated by Raymond P. Scheindlin (Philadelphia: Jewish Publication Society. New York: Jewish Theological Seminary of America, 1993). On Orthodox liturgy: Jean Danielou, *The Bible and the Liturgy*, Liturgical Studies, 3 (Notre Dame, Ind.: University of Notre Dame, 1956), Alexander Schmemann, *Great Lent: Journey to Pascha* (Crestwood, N.Y.: St. Vladimir's Seminary Press, 1969), Georges Barrois, *Scripture Readings in Orthodox Worship* (Crestwood, N.Y.: St. Vladimir's Seminary Press, 1977), and *The Lenten Triodion*, translated by Mother Mary and Kallistos Ware (London: Faber and Faber, 1977). On the modern lectionaries and their problems: William Skudlarek, *The Word in Worship: Preaching in a Liturgical Context*, Abingdon Preacher's Library (Nashville: Abingdon, 1981), and Gail Ramshaw, *Christ in Sacred Speech: The Meaning of Liturgical Language* (Philadelphia: Fortress, 1986).

What

"MODERN"

BIBLICAL STUDIES DO

THE STUDY OF THE BIBLE HAS TAKEN NUMEROUS FORMS THROUGHOUT history. When Europe emerged from the Renaissance, its academic centers turned their attention to empirical studies of nearly everything. Scientific questions were asked of natural, mechanical, political, and philosophical aspects of civilization. Not surprisingly, some people began to raise questions about the theological presuppositions of their culture, the Bible included. The use of scientific methods to investigate the contents and the history of the Bible has come to be known as "higher criticism." Through its various methods, higher criticism has attempted to find answers to particular questions asked of the biblical texts; in this it also removes from its concern other areas of biblical meaning. This is a problem that has long been pointed out by Bible scholars not engaged in higher criticism but only recently understood by the higher critics themselves.

Those who engage in modern "higher critical" studies are overwhelmingly religious scholars. Though many Jewish and Christian communities view these methods of research as heretical, for the most part these approaches have become the methodologies of mainline and liberal branches of Protestant and Catholic Christianity and of Reformed Judaism. As the twentieth century closes, a number of conservative and Orthodox Christian communities, who traditionally have been wary of this scholarship, have entered into selected areas of higher critical research as well.

It needs to be understood from the start that "modern" biblical studies did not begin at any given point in time; the questions these studies ask of the biblical texts (as well as of the Jewish and Christian traditions themselves) have been around from the beginning of the respective religions. However, if one wished to pick a time that could be usefully (if not quite accurately) cited for the origin of modern Bible research, the late seventeenth century would be that time. Modern scholarly investigation of the Bible has been said to begin with the observations made by Benedictus de Spinoza (1632–1677) and Richard Simon (1638–1712) to the effect that the Pentateuch of the Old Testament was composed of several different narratives that came from different authors and were, in their current form, repetitive. By questioning the traditional belief that Moses had written the first five books of the Bible, both scholars took leave of the traditional beliefs of their respective religious communities.

Forerunners

Modern higher critical research was built upon earlier areas of study, three of which are of particular interest. Prior to the development of those fields considered to be part of higher criticism, there was intensive investigation concerning the origins of the biblical text itself. Textual criticism was already well-established before the Protestant Reformation and is pursued by most Western Christian traditions to this day (see chapter 3). The intent of the Textual Critics was originally to reconstruct the most accurate Greek text of the Bible possible (for the earliest textual studies were concentrated on the New Testament text). To do this the various manuscripts with their varying textual contents were compared and, through a series of criteria, an accepted Greek text was proposed as the best textual reconstruction. Since there are numerous early New Testament manuscripts and none of them agree on the exact content of any given book, every Christian community, whether aware of it or not, is dependent on textual critics to produce the New Testament that they read as "the Bible."

The second, source criticism, is generally accepted as the earliest "higher" critical study of the Bible. It began simply as an attempt to discern the duplicate stories in the Pentateuch and the differences in literary style that could be found. The early scholars asked Why should the story of Abraham have two stories of the Patriarch telling someone else that his wife is his sister, such that she is taken by that other person for his own wife, or why does Hagar get sent out into the desert twice in very similar stories? The answer that was given was that there were two different sources that had told the same stories each in its own way, but both tales had been preserved.

The identification of the biblical sources themselves began in earnest with the French physician and sometime Bible scholar Jean Astruc (1684–1766), who in 1753 published a study in which he demonstrated that the creation story of Genesis was really two different stories by two different authors with different styles and different names used for God. From this observation, he could name one author the Elohist (Elohim = "God") and the other the Yahwist (Yahweh = the name of God) on the basis of the word written to refer to God. The writing styles, theology, and vision of the world of each writer was clear and distinct. By the nineteenth century four "sources" had been discovered in the Pentateuch: Yahwist, Elohist, Priestly, and Deuteronomist. Each source had its own distinctive characteristics and usually could be easily spotted in the narratives.

The search for sources expanded into other books of the Old Testament beyond the Torah. Julius Wellhausen (1844–1918) attempted to provide a chronological history of the various sources as they originally had been added together to form the Bible texts that now exist. Wellhausen's work provoked a number of responses, ranging from wholehearted acceptance to total rejection; however, the search for the sources of the Bible continued into the twentieth century, with elaborate theories proposed to determine the origins of individual sentences, even words, within the biblical books.

The third foundational critical study was that of history. Historical critical studies began almost as soon as there were biblical texts to be read. Early Jewish and Christian scholars made chronologies and wrote narratives that combined classical Greek and Roman histories with the Bible. Modern history, as an attempt to be dispassionate and objective, however, is a product of the last couple of centuries. Basic to modern historical studies are a series of notions that were not part of the ancient world. Foremost among these notions is that history is a human endeavor; neither divine intervention nor miraculous event is allowed in historical reconstruction. Another standard aspect of modern historical studies is the constant questioning of the sources as to author, purpose, and biases. Until the early nineteenth century the Bible remained the most important source for ancient history; but now the reconstructions of ancient Near Eastern history are composed mostly from material uncovered by archaeological excavations in Mesopotamia or Egypt. However, the Bible remains the most important source for the history of the early church and ancient Judah and Israel. The correspondence between the history that appears in the Bible and the ancient history as reconstructed by modern Bible historians has never been entirely clear and remains diverse among scholars (see chapter 8).

Form Criticism

Extensive research into the form of narrative units began in Germany late in the nineteenth century as a reaction to the source critical tendency to subdivide biblical texts into ever-smaller units. Hermann Gunkel (1862–1932) is usually credited with beginning form studies in Old Testament scholarship. Using contemporary research into folk literature (European interest in collecting folk tales was at its height in the second half of the nineteenth century), Gunkel posited that the narratives of the Bible (including the Pentateuch) fit into standard folkloric forms rather than necessarily reflecting numerous sources.

It was soon noted that particular types of literature had set literary formulas, structures, and vocabulary. Gunkel, and those doing form critical studies since him, have set out to classify the forms in which biblical texts appear. New Testament forms, like "epistle" or "gospel" were fairly clear; however, Old Testament forms have had to be uncovered from the texts and from comparative literature recovered from the ancient Near East. The various forms of the psalms were defined to a large extent by Gunkel himself. Once the basic formula for a "hymn" was described it, became clear that the "form" was common throughout the ancient Near East. A hymn, by the way, has this form (using Psalm 29 as an example):

Introductory call to praise God	vs. 1–2
Thematic sentence	v. 3a
Hymn of Praise	vs. 3b–9
Concluding verse	vs. 10–11

Numerous forms and subforms have been described for the biblical texts, such as the "Woe Oracles" in prophecy (a condemnation of a nation by a deity through a prophet, found throughout the ancient world; see Amos 1–2) or "Call Narratives" in biographies (a teacher calling a disciple with a phrase used as a strange twist, not only found in the Gospels, but also in classical biographies of philosophers; see Matthew 4:18–22). Form criticism first seeks to classify passages in the Bible according to their literary structure.

Once the form is determined, the second concern of the form critic is to place the passage in its *Sitz im Leben* ("Situation in Life" is a German term used by scholars to refer to the place and purpose a document fills in a culture). For example, creation stories in the ancient Near East tended to be part of New Year ceremonies. Or, in the New Testament, Hebrews can be shown to be a sermon of a category derived from a particular type of rabbinic interpretation. Knowing that particular forms of literature were used in particular situations suggested to the scholars how the texts originally might have been used, such that the first chapters of Genesis may have been composed for the Jewish New Year and that Hebrews was a homily presented for the Lord's Day service.

Once the situation of the text has been determined, the third task of the form critic is to compare the biblical passage with other examples of similar literature of the same form from the literature or inscriptions of the ancient world. Once ancient creation myths were investigated, it could be asserted that the ceremonies in which they were recited celebrated the establishing of the "current" ruler on the throne to keep order for the deities and so served to legitimate the dynasty already in control. Genesis' creation stories have been so read. In the case of Hebrews, knowing that the work was a homily based on scripture allowed scholars to realize that the model for the argument that runs through the text comes from Jewish biblical exegesis and probably derives from Synagogue sermons.

Form critical studies can answer numerous questions, but they can raise many others. In the psalms it is not uncommon to find God compared to other deities as being greater than all other gods; however, there are not supposed to be any other gods in the biblical worldview. Once one looks at hymns written to other deities of the ancient world, one realizes that the phrase is a stock formula found in hymns, which the biblical authors have used because it is part of the "form" of a hymn. The Jewish or Christian reader can dismiss the reference to other gods as a figure of speech. Yet, when Paul in his letters lists virtues and vices, does this mean Christians are bound by these lists? Traditionally the moral admonitions of

Paul have been taken as guides to Christian living. However, the form critical study of the Greek letter shows that these lists are a formulaic part of a letter* (First Thessalonians as an example):

Opening:	Sender	1:1a
	Addressee	1:1b
	Greeting	1:1c
Thanksgiving/Blessing		1:2–10
Body of the letter		2:1–5:11
*Paraenesis (=traditional moral advice)		5:12–22
Closing:	Wish for health	5:23
	Farewell	5:26–28

Generally, the moral admonitions are stock lists (often from Stoic philosophy in Paul's case). One can still read the lists as moral admonitions from Paul, though one can just as easily treat the lists simply as a stock part of a letter with no more inherent content than the standard American letter formula, "Dear...," which may begin anything from a love letter to a lawsuit.

Form criticism works best where the forms are clear and well-attested, like the New Testament letters. Form criticism becomes less certain when the form is not well-attested or contains aspects of several formulas. The Gospels, for example, bear close affinities with Greco-Roman biography but also contain large formulas from the Old Testament and the rabbinic Jewish world. It is easier to explain, for example, the Call Narrative statement "I will make you fishers of humans" than it is to explain the gospel narratives as a whole from this scholarly approach.

Redaction History

A second response to source criticism was "redaction history." If the Bible is made up of sources, then how were those sources handed down through the religious tradition to become the Bible texts that we now have? At first, the concern of this branch of study was the movement from oral tradition to written text, but it has expanded to include the transmission of the written text as well. Though the Old Testament redaction history scholars worked on the reconstruction of the manner by which oral history was passed on to scribes, it may be easier to understand the problems of redaction history if the sayings of Jesus are used for an example.

The questions that have been asked in this branch of higher criticism usually come from devout Christians seeking the actual words of Jesus. In a sense the quest has been to find the Word of God behind the Bible as "word of God," assuming that Jesus' exact sayings would be more authoritative than the scriptures that now carry the message as spoken by Jesus.

The search begins from the simple observation that Jesus, in all probability, did not speak Greek, but either Hebrew or Aramaic, as most Jews in the areas of Judea and Galilee are assumed to have known at that time. So one of the first debates in New Testament redaction history has been about what language Jesus spoke. Assuming he was like other rabbis, he spoke Hebrew (or Aramaic) when teaching. So, if one begins with the words spoken by Jesus to his disciples, the words were not Greek. The record we have of these words, however, is in Greek, because that was the language of the early church. How, then, did the Hebrew/Aramaic sayings of Jesus become New Testament Greek?

Since Jesus is not recorded, or even reported, as having written down his own sayings, they must have been recorded by others. A short chain of those passing on the material can be constructed. The argument would run something like the following.

Someone who heard Jesus speak wrote the very words down soon after he heard them. Now, for those who hold the Gospels of John and Matthew to have been written by the disciples of those names, this would explain the direct connection (not the change in language, but the accuracy of the quotations). However, most higher critics doubt that any of the disciples wrote down the sayings of Jesus. For one thing, Jesus taught as a rabbi, and at that time Jewish rabbis passed down their teachings orally to their disciples, who then, in turn, passed them on orally to their own disciples. It was the Greek tradition that wanted written texts of the wise sayings of the teacher.

The followers of Jesus, a group larger than the disciples, no doubt talked among themselves about what Jesus had said. The oral tradition worked out a sort of hierarchy of importance concerning the sayings of Jesus. Most of what Jesus said in his life was not of any importance to them. For example, they did not discuss everyday speech (you will look in vain in the biblical texts for Jesus to say, "Please pass the matzo," even though he is as certain to have actually said that at some point in his life as anything recorded in the Gospels); it just was not important for the early church.

The sayings that were passed on were those that were understood to contain Jesus' teachings. Those sayings most clearly bearing the message that the church understood as central to Jesus' message became the most discussed. As the early Christians met on the Lord's Day to celebrate the memory of Jesus, the most important sayings became the basis for their homilies (patterned on the homilies in the synagogues, in which they were still faithful members). The usual wisdom of the origins of the recorded sayings of Jesus is that someone/some people went about collecting the various sayings of Jesus from the various Christian meeting places, or from those who had heard Jesus speak. This person, or these persons, then sorted out the sayings and wrote down those considered most important to them, producing a written text of Jesus' sayings (usually called "Q" from the German "Quelle" [="source" meaning the sayings of Jesus source]). This text was probably already written in Greek, so the collector(s) may have done his/her/their own translating. This means that the understanding of the sayings as the collector read them became normative for the sayings that appear in the Gospels of Matthew and Luke, each of whom is supposed to have had a copy of this collection (Mark may or may not have had a copy; it's being fought over by scholars at the moment).

Redaction criticism has taken all passages of the Bible and attempted to do much the same sort of reconstruction with them. The basic problem for redactional studies is the manner by which original material arrives as the text that now appears in the Bible.

Tradition History

Another early higher criticism was the attempt to follow certain motifs that reappear in the Bible in a historical procession. The "traditions" were major events or theological ideas that reappear in the Bible through a series of texts that can be placed in some chronological order. As created, tradition history did not deal with phrases or formulas but with significant events.

Probably the central event that could be traced out in its reinterpretation through the Bible was the exodus. Ignoring, for the moment, the problems with reconstructing the historical chronology of the passages, a traditional outline sketch of the tradition history of the exodus could be reconstructed in the following manner (keeping in mind that many scholars find this reconstruction either too conservative or too liberal):

The exodus event itself was experienced, but it was not written down until the time of the Kingdom of David or Solomon when one formulation of the narrative was produced as a support for the dynasty of David. Another rendition of the same event was written in the kingdom of Israel when the two kingdoms of Judah and Israel split apart so that the northern kingdom would have its own version more favorable to its own territory. The prophet Hosea (11:1–4), a century later, picks up the motif and uses it to condemn the behavior of Israel in his own day. It would also be used by Jeremiah (16:14–18) a century after that for much the same purpose against Judah. The prophet, called Second Isaiah, who wrote in the Babylonian exile, however, took up the exodus tradition and used it to soothe the fears of the Judeans living in Mesopotamia; now it was a second exodus that brought hope (40). Paul picks up the exodus motif (1 Corinthians 10:1–13) to warn Christians about slipping away from the faith they had found; whereas Hebrews (3:1–19) uses the exodus to show that Jesus is a mightier savior than was Moses.

Classic examples of tradition history can be found for creation, patriarchal narratives, the Kingdom of David, and the covenant with God. Tradition history deals mainly with the biblical texts themselves, but has more recently been extended into early Jewish literature and Christian writings outside the canon. One can theoretically carry a study of a tradition right up to the modern church or synagogue (or, in some instances, the mosque).

Literary Criticism

There are a large number of approaches to the Bible that fall under the heading of literary criticism. In all its forms, this approach seeks to use the latest in critical thought to read the biblical text. At first, literary criticism was used to understand the large sections of biblical books in a manner similar to reading other forms of literature. To this end, various types of literature were compared to Biblical texts. Old Testament historical narratives have gone through periods of intensive comparison with ancient Greek histories, Icelandic Norse epics, Hungarian folk history, Slavic fairy tales, and Mesopotamian royal inscriptions. New Testament Gospels and the Acts have been more restricted in their comparative study to Greek and Latin literature.

One major discovery through literary studies has been the realization that large sections of narrative have their own structures, often incorporating earlier material but having their own literary coherence. The duplicate "sources" of Genesis in the story of Abraham become less obvious once one knows that *chiastic* ordering was common in both Greek and Hebrew literature. Chiasm simply describes a literary order that duplicates narrative, or select words, on either side of a central point in the story or poem. The Abraham cycle, read through a chiastic structure, becomes a coherent narrative, with its emphasis on the covenent made between God and Abraham/Sarah in chapter 17:

> A Abraham called by God (to leave Haran)
> B Denial of Sarai as wife (Egypt)
>   C Rescue of Lot (from the five kings of the East)
>   D Hagar sent away
>   E Covenant with Abram and Sarai
>   (Abraham and Sarah)
>   C' Rescue of Lot (from Sodom)
>   B' Denial of Sarah as wife (Gerar)
> D' Hagar sent away
> A' Abraham called by God (to sacrifice Isaac)

Similar structures have been found in numerous texts of the Bible, including the Gospel of Matthew and the Jacob stories of Genesis. Other standard forms of narrative construction have been recovered from ancient literatures, showing that biblical texts had more continuity than the Source Critics had suggested.

Literary criticism also introduced into the study of the Bible modern questions concerning reading texts. Since the understanding of the person reading the text determines what the text says, numerous branches of literary studies have investigated the manner by which we know what we read. A couple of examples may help clarify what these studies attempt to explain. "Structuralists" attempt to demonstrate that the literary construction of a world is built on the understanding of the authors of the text according to the relation of significant aspects of the world as they knew it. Everything that appears in the text can be related to the notions of society, good and evil, cosmology, honor and shame, and so forth (usually done in studies by investigating opposites); however, readers understand the texts in the context of their own world structures, which are not those of the authors, making the text say something different (at least to an extent) to each reader. Reader response studies deal precisely with the questions raised by what it is that people read when they read a text. Such mundane questions as why people read the Bible at all, what they expect to find in it, what they assume they are reading, and how much of what they understand as coming from the text comes instead from their own filling-in of material not in the text they are reading are investigated in this research. In short, everyone reads her or his own text out of the Bible. These studies lead eventually into the whole area of linguistic philosophy; how do words mean anything?

Hermeneutics

The study of hermeneutics was early despised by some communities, which held that the Bible could only mean one thing. The purpose of hermeneutical studies is to recover and explain the various meanings that people and groups have found in the texts through time and traditions (see chapter 5). In more recent times, hermeneutic studies has been adapted into the notion of "multiculturalism," so that the various interpretations of Bible passages are seen as on the same level of importance. It has been stressed not only that one ought to know the various historical interpretations, but that all the schools of Bible studies in the world need to be acknowledged. In practice, this usually means that one does stress a particular form of interpretation (or a few) over most of the others.

Currently, the hermeneutical sphere of study has moved into the actual production of various interpretations of scripture from particular readers' views. So there are Liberation Bible studies, black-theology interpretations, Latin American, African, Chicano, Korean, South Asian, feminist, and numerous other biblical interpretations being developed. Since the reading of the text, as it affects the reader in this world and in the practice of one's life, becomes the center of importance, the meaning of the original author becomes less important (or even of no importance). The result of this emphasis on using the texts rather than recovering early meanings of them has been to cause the higher critical study of the Bible to move from the center of scholarly concern to the margins of study.

A Word about Feminist Bible Studies

A major approach to biblical studies at the moment falls under the heading "feminist"; however, this title covers a vast array of opinions and methods. Any form of Bible criticism may be engaged from a feminist standpoint. At one extreme, feminist Bible scholars attempt to recover the lives of the women of the biblical world. Since the Bible stories center on male figures, the lives and importance of women need to be reconstructed from very little data; often the texts make it clear that women were of greater importance than the current narratives display. In these cases feminist scholars want not only to recover the stories of the women, but to find out why the authors marginalized them. At the other extreme are feminists who wish to demonstrate why the Bible, as a male-written text supporting a hierarchical world run by and for men should be rejected by everyone, especially women. For these scholars the authoritarian, oppressive society the Bible reflects cannot be used in any form to construct a just and equitable society. The marginalization of women in the biblical texts is seen as central to the Bible's message, and, therefore, the Bible and the religions deriving from it are evil, needing to be destroyed in order to create a better world.

Most feminist scholars engaged in Bible studies fall between these two extremes; however, central to all feminist studies is the need to position the views of women in the place of most importance in reading the texts. Feminist scholarship may take up anything from textual criticism to reader response. Historical reconstructions of the ancient world, intentions of the authors, understandings of the early readers, use by church and synagogue leaders, and the psychological effect on women who read the texts all tend to become important for feminist scholars of all types. Reading texts with a particular view toward the material makes possible numerous observations of great value not only for understanding the texts, but for understanding the readers, making the history and the content of the texts clearer. The most important aspect of the feminist study of biblical texts is to demonstrate the equality of men and women both in scholarship and in the religious communities that use the texts. Many religious communities that do not allow women positions of standing in the decision-making process or in interpreting scripture have found all feminist positions to be unacceptable, whereas many Protestant and some Catholic communities have been affected by feminist research in both practice and theory.

Questions for Reflection and Discussion
1. Most Christians use some aspects of higher criticism and reject others. What sorts of questions do you have that higher critics investigate? Are there questions in which you are not interested?

2. Higher criticism was largely a product of North European Protestantism; do the studies that these scholars produce have any bearing on any other religious group. Should they?

3. Most higher scholarly research held a notion that some sort of "reality" could be determined through their approaches; currently, there is a wide belief that there is no reality beyond the culture in which some shared notion of reality is accepted. Can higher critical studies be taken seriously in a world in which the majority of people reject its very premise?

4. What kinds of questions would you like answered about the Bible, and can you imagine how to go about discovering the answers to them?

5. Attempt to read the Garden of Eden story (Genesis 2:4b–3:24) through various feminist eyes. How can the text be read to highlight the positive status of women? How can it be read to show that the Bible should be abandoned? How many ways can the passage be interpreted?

Bibliography

The best series of introductions to the various forms of modern Bible scholarship are the Old and New Testament series of the Guides of Biblical Scholarship, published by Fortress Press; these deal in depth, but at a readable level, with the major approaches to the Bible in use today. A survey of major figures in the development of "modern" biblical studies is presented in Roy A. Harrisville and Walter Sundberg, *The Bible in Modern Culture: Theology and HIstorical-Critical Method from Spinoza to Käsemann* (Grand Rapids: Wm. B. Eerdmans, 1995). Two of the classics of feminist Bible scholarship are: Phyllis Trible, *God and the Rhetoric of Sexuality* (Philadelphia: Fortress, 1978), and Elisabeth Schüssler Fiorenza, *In Memory of Her: A Feminist Theological Reconstruction of Christian Origins* (New York: Crossroad, 1983).

THE BIBLE
AND THE QUR'AN

JUDAISM, CHRISTIANITY, AND ISLAM SHARE A RELIGIOUS TRADITION. While the Tanak of Judaism is incorporated into Christian Bibles, the Qur'an (also spelled *Koran*) the holy book of Islam, does not incorporate the texts of the Bible. However, persons and narratives from the Jewish and Christian holy books are found in the Qur'an. Though the sacred text of Islam contains much material that is similar to portions of the Christian Bible, it should be noted that the Islamic attitude toward its sacred scripture is somewhat different than that of Christianity or Judaism toward their sacred texts.

There is no real reason to doubt the belief, held sacred by Muslims, that Muhammad (ca. 570–629 C.E.) recited the entire contents of the Qur'an in 114 poetic *surahs* (books) ranging from the extensive "Cow" to *surahs* of only a verse in length. The poetic recitations came at unexpected times over several years. These recitations were written down, according to tradition, at the time Muhammad spoke them by those in the immediate company of Muhammad and on whatever was available at the moment, including camel bones and scraps of cloth. The collection that now appears as the Qur'an was edited by Abu Bakr within the lifetime of Muhammad, according to Islamic tradition.

Islam holds that the true religion has been revealed to humans through numerous prophets over many years. The divine revelation provided to humanity comes from a single sacred book kept in heaven. It is the understanding of Islamic faith that the Jewish Tanak and the Christian Bible (sometimes referred to as "Torah and Gospel" in Islam) are derived from the same holy book in heaven from which came the Qur'an. Jews and Christians are believed to have altered the texts that they were given by God through misunderstanding and human copying errors. The Qur'an is argued to be free from errors of understanding or copying because God had the angel Gabriel dictate the contents directly to Muhammad and he, in turn, is believed to have overseen the production of the collected texts. The claim that the other religions have corrupted their sacred texts has been a common argument of Jews, Christians, and Muslims in interreligious debates for centuries.

The text of the Qur'an has been standardized since the third generation of Islam; at that time one copy was selected as authoritative on the basis of the reliability of those who had produced it. All Qur'ans now contain the same text down to the last letter. In order to avoid the problems that early Muslims could see in the traditions of their Jewish and Christian neighbors, it was determined that only the Arabic original could be cited as authoritative when using the Qur'an; this avoided the innumerable problems Jews and Christians have had with translating their sacred texts into other languages.

The Qur'an tends to deal with issues and not narratives. It is an Islamic belief that the heavenly original of the book has all entries in order and in narrative form, but that the revelations given to Muhammad were presented in such a fashion that the meaning intended to be learned from the texts would be clear. All who attain heaven, it is said, will be able to read the original book in its true form. In the meantime, the various books of the faithful communities (including Jews and Christians) should allow them to understand the desire of God and explain to them how to submit to divine will.

Narratives

The clear tradition of Jewish and Christian biblical narrative in the Qur'an makes it important that Christians be aware of the connection between their own holy book and the Muslim sacred text. Most Qur'anic scholars, in fact, have some knowledge of the Bible, so it would be nice if Bible scholars had some knowledge of the Qur'an, though most do not. Here a few comments about similar materials in the religious traditions' holy books are followed by ten biblical characters as they appear in the Qur'an.

Some of the surahs have names that will sound familiar to Christians from characters in their own Bibles. Surah titles include "Joseph" (which indeed relates the story of Joseph much as it appears in Genesis 37–50, with a few major differences), "Abraham" (only one of numerous places in the Qur'an where the faith of Abraham is described), "Noah" (which tells the story of the flood), and "Mary" (which relates the story of Mary's piety and God's granting her a son). The only surah that has the same name as a book in the Bible is "Jonah." The basic story of Jonah is essentially the same in Islam as it is in Judaism and Christianity; however, the story is told differently and is used to display the manner by which the true prophet can overcome any danger because God protects those who submit to the true faith and speak the truth against all odds.

The historical world presented in the Qur'an derives both from Arabian culture and the biblical rendition of history. The creation of the world is followed by the creation of Adam, the rise of numerous peoples, and the calling of Abraham to the obedient life of a follower of God. The two sons of Abraham, Ishmael and Isaac, are both destined to be the ancestors of believing peoples. Ishmael is the origin of the Arab peoples who take up Islam from Muhammad, and Isaac is the first of the Israelites who are presented with God's revelation but can only partially grasp it. Christians come from the Jewish tradition but mistake their prophet for their deity.

God is presented as all powerful, all knowing, and the creator of the entire earth and all its inhabitants. Though English writers often use the name *Allah* to refer to God within the faith of Islam, the word *Allah* is the Arabic word for "God" and so refers to the same deity as appears in the Bible in Hebrew as *El* or Greek as *Theos*; in English we translate both biblical words as "God." God in the Qur'an may interfere with history on behalf of humans or to punish the wicked, in much the same manner as appears in the Bible.

Adam

The first human created is called Adam. He is made by God to be the crowning achievement of creation and is, therefore, considered to be good and righteous. The purpose of humans was to serve as God's personal rulers over the earth. Upon creation of the first person, God called the angels to come see the new creature. So pleased was God with the human that a divine request was made that they bow to Adam as he named each individual angel. This they all did, save for Iblis ("devil" = Satan [who is often understood in Islamic commentary to have been a jinn and not an angel]), who refused to acknowledge that people could be greater than angels (or at least himself); this is seen as the fall of Satan from the grace of God. God provided a garden for Adam to live in, but Iblis set out to distract Adam and all humans in coming generations from the ways of God.

Adam and his wife (Eve is not named in the Qur'an) are settled by God in the garden and told not to go near the tree in the middle of the garden. Iblis immediately set out to cause them to disobey God's regulation and was successful. Though Adam and his wife had to leave the garden, God continued to give them guidance so that their lives could be lived in harmony with God. The Qur'anic vision of humans is that they are created and continue to be basically good creatures and held high in God's favor.

Noah

Noah is presented as a prophet who lived in a time when people had listened to Iblis and the entire earth had become filled with wickedness. God, always attempting to save everyone, reveals his message to Noah, a righteous man. Noah preaches and preaches to his neighbors, but they refuse to believe him and only become more evil. The point is reached when it is necessary for God to destroy these evil persons. Since it is a basic premise of the Qur'an that God saves true prophets, God instructs Noah to build a boat for himself, his family, and the creatures. Those who are wicked and refuse to repent, even when offered the chance several times, are destroyed in a great flood. Noah is saved to repopulate the world.

Abraham

It is no exaggeration to say that Abraham is the hero of the Qur'an. In both Judaism and Christianity Abraham is presented as the classic example of the faithful person; this is emphasized in the Qur'an. Neither a Jew nor a Christian, Abraham is shown to be one who submits entirely to the will of God and therefore is the first true Muslim ("one who submits"). The story of Abraham's turning from his father's idols when he was a boy living in Mesopotamia and accepting the one true God as it is told in the Qur'an has its parallel, not in biblical texts, but in Jewish haggadah (expansions of the Bible tales). Abraham and his son Ishmael are presented establishing the holy center of Mecca, to which pilgrimage is required of Muslims. Ishmael is the chosen favorite of Abraham, but God blesses both sons, Isaac and Ishmael.

The story of the attempted sacrifice of Isaac, which appears in Genesis 22, also appears in the Qur'an. However, it is fundamental to Islamic faith that God does not order people to do evil. Since human sacrifice is forbidden, God could not have ordered Abraham to sacrifice Isaac. In the Qur'an it is a dream that causes Abraham to believe that God has requested the slaying of his son. God intervenes in time to save Isaac and to instruct Abraham on the need to distinguish true divine revelation from one's own imagination.

Abraham is seen as a prophet who delivers the message of God to his contemporaries while at the same time living a life that allows people to learn the life of a devout believer by imitation. The Qur'an continuously stresses the need for people not to become attached to names, or books, or traditions, but to be like Abraham, one who submitted directly to the will of God.

Ishmael

A word about Ishmael is probably important. In the Bible Ishmael is Abraham's first son, and the father desires that he be the child of the promise, but God insists the son of Sarah will be the bearer of the blessing. Ishmael and his mother, Hagar (who is not named in the Qur'an), are sent off into the desert, where they become the founders of all the Arabian peoples. In the Qur'an Abraham maintains his devotion to Ishmael. Since the origins of Islam are in Arabia, it is not strange that the founder of the Arabian peoples becomes Abraham's central child.

Ishmael is presented as a perfect Muslim, as was his father Abraham. The two of them found the central shrine of Islam, and his descendants will make up the core of the faithful. It is Ishmael's lineage that falls away from the faith, to which Muhammad was called to return them.

Moses

At no point does the Qur'an tell the exodus story in one narrative. However, almost the entire biblical episode appears scattered throughout the surahs. Though of humble beginnings, Moses is a major prophet, who is required to preach the truth to Pharaoh in Egypt. Pharaoh is not interested, being himself too proud of his own power. The Pharaoh, indeed, sets himself up to counter the truth itself, and this ends in disaster for him. The punishment of Egypt comes because of the disdain in which the Egyptians hold the word of God as spoken by the true prophet.

Moses is called by a voice from a burning bush to deliver the message of God to the Israelites; the staff turning into a snake episode also appears here as it does in the Bible. Moses brings a thorough teaching of the message of God, but the people do not take it entirely to heart. Nonetheless, they are saved from Egyptian slavery by the power of God that has been accepted by Moses. Though Moses is regarded as a great believer, he demonstrates that one cannot always have success in communicating God's message to others simply because one's own faith is great.

In the surah called "The Cave," a story is told of Moses that is unique to the Qur'an. Here Moses meets a spiritual believer who is much advanced over Moses in his devotion to God. In a series of three incidents Moses displays his misunderstanding of the insight of the superior believer and finally acknowledges that he is not yet capable of being this man's disciple.

David

The traditions of David as king, poet, and prophet are stressed in the Qur'an. The story of David and Goliath is related, though in a very shortened form; it is not clear that David is understood to be a child. Saul's army confronts the giant and David is the warrior who defeats him. As ruler, David is considered a just and pious ruler, yet needing armor to fight the unbelievers surrounding his nation, so that God shows him how to make iron-mail suits of armor. As with the Jewish tradition of David as the author of the book of Psalms, David is understood to have written numerous songs in praise of God. God also teaches revelation to David such that he is a great prophet, a notion that appears to have come from early Christian use of the psalms as prophetic texts (an interpretation that had appeared already in the New Testament).

The court case from the famous story in Second Samuel 12:1–15 of Nathan tricking David into condemning himself over his adultery with Bathsheba appears in the Qur'an mightily transformed. Here the case is presented as a real case brought by two men, one with ninety-nine ewes and one with only one; the wealthy man stole the poor man's single item of livestock. David decides in favor of the poor man. There is no notion of David having been guilty of anything in this rendition of the story. Indeed, the more question-able behavior of David as he appears in the Bible is missing alto-gether from the Qur'an, reflecting more the character of the Israelite king as he appears in Chronicles and in Jewish and Christian tradi-tional literature than in the Books of Samuel.

Solomon

Solomon takes up a more distinguished position in Islamic tra-dition than he has in either Judaism or Christianity. A prophet, like his father David, he is also wise. A recurring motif in Solomon legends, already to be found in the Qur'an, is his knowledge of the speech of birds (and other animals). The magical traditions con-cerning Solomon, which appear throughout the classical world in late antiquity, are also found in the Solomon of Islam. Solomon controls the wind because God has given him this power. More-over, he has jinn (genies) at his beck and call.

The longest story told of Solomon in the Qur'an concerns the visit by the Queen of Sheba. Solomon hears of her kingdom, a place where people, under the influence of Iblis, worship the sun. Solomon sends the queen a letter offering to convert her and her people to the true religion. She tests him by offering vast riches, thinking that if he takes them he is merely greedy, but if he rejects them, then he is a true prophet. He, of course, rejects them. She decides to visit him, but to impress her Solomon has his jinn bring her own throne to his palace so that she might see the power that being a believer entails. He also, through his magic, causes the floor to become a body of water, covered by clear glass so that she raises up her clothing to keep it from getting wet, unaware that she is safely above it (this is a popular Qur'anic story retold several times in Muslim literary traditions).

The wealth, wisdom, piety, magic, and building activities of Solomon are all mentioned in the sacred text. Many legends con-cerning each of these aspects of Solomon have been produced in commentaries on the Qur'an and in popular culture. Solomon is seen as the ideal of the ruler and a ruler understood to have ruled both east and west with wisdom, justice, and submission to God.

Job

There is no great long book or narrative about Job in the Qur'an. The Jewish Hebrew story of Job that appears in the Bible is compli-cated and convoluted; it was somewhat simplified in its translation into Greek and Latin in the Christian tradition, but in the Qur'an Job is noted only as a true prophet who demonstrates the power of God. The righteous Job is selected by God to have the true religion revealed to him, that he may teach it to his contemporaries. However, Iblis, seeking to cause him to cease teaching and disbelieve God, afflicts Job with terrible suffering. However, Job, who is patient as in Christian tradition (James 5:11), calls for aid from God, and God removes all the afflictions tormenting him. Thus, we are taught that true prophets are protected by God.

Mary

It usually comes as a bit of a surprise to Christians (let alone Jews) that the Qur'an holds Mary in deep veneration. She has a surah named after her, which tells her story and some of that of her son, the prophet Jesus. While Christians contemporary with Muhammad did hold Mary in special regard, high Christian Mariology was a half-millennium in the future at the time the surahs of the Qur'an were recited. Mary is portrayed as a virtuous woman with deep faith in God. Due to her moral behavior and her deep submission to God, God granted her a child who was to be one of the greatest of all prophets. Though she had not had sexual relations with a man, she had a son by means of the divine will. It should be noted that Muslim scholars point out that this is not to be understood in the same manner as the Christian notion of the virgin birth. The point here is that God can do anything, and God does act for those who are truly devoted to the true faith.

Jesus

For Christians in most denominations Jesus is known as Christ, the second person of the Trinity. This is a theological point that the Qur'an addresses directly. For the Qur'an, Jesus was the greatest prophet next to Muhammad, but he was a human prophet, directed by God. The notion of Jesus as divine is understood in the Qur'an to be a classic example of Christians misunderstanding their own revelation and slipping away from monotheism into polytheism.

Jesus was called by God to heal and teach; he called apostles to help him bring other people to faith in God and prepare them for the coming resurrection day. He was born of Mary already set aside for the work of a prophet, such that his entire life was devoted to the propagation of the faith. So effective was his message that those who were evil sought him out and crucified him; but God, always saving the faithful, took Jesus away as they nailed him to the cross so that only an empty husk was actually executed. He was a mighty prophet who saved many people, but his message was twisted by some of his followers, so that many Christians worship the prophet rather than the true faith in God that he had taught them.

Theology

Like the biblical God, the Qur'anic God is the power behind all of creation. The Qur'an seeks to teach people to recognize that God created everything and therefore everything that exists is dependent on God as the ultimate source for its being and sustenance. Since God created all the laws of nature, and God wishes people to live happily in the world, humans are capable of understanding the natural world. Traditionally, Islam has stressed that the natural sciences are never at odds with the revelation of the Qur'an. Moreover, the social sciences (history, sociology, and anthropology) have long traditions in Islamic learning, grounded already in the teachings of the Qur'an that urge believers to study humanity and society as a means of understanding the ways of God.

Humans, in the Qur'an, are understood to have been created good. The basic instinct of all people is to obey God, though human nature may lead individuals astray, or Iblis may tempt persons to disobey God. The natural world has been put under the dominion of humanity, but persons are expected to treat it with the care with which God created it. Offenses by humans against God are generally forgiven by God so long as the entirety of a human's life is lived well; the mercy of God is stressed both in text and tradition. The worst characteristic one may have is greed, for it harms not only the individual person, but also society and nature. It is the duty of all persons to make their way in the world: work is expected of all to their own capacity; however, the work must be for the good of society, and profits must be shared with those less fortunate. It is the duty of all good Muslims to strive for the alleviation of poverty, suffering, and need.

Revelation of the divine will is offered to humanity by way of a series of prophets. These prophets have been selected and protected by God to allow all peoples to live in a manner pleasing to God and in harmony with each other. The Jewish and Christian Bibles are undestood to carry part of the revelation. The Qur'an is understood to carry a more complete revelation, but in and of itself it is not the same as full revelation, which remains for the faithful in the heavenly book. It is stated that those who do not believe in the revelation of God will remain opposed to the true faith and in conflict with those who believe until the final days.

There is an end judgment coming. Like the Judaism of the late Roman period and many traditions in Christianity, most strands of Islam believe in the final judgment of the individual human souls by God. The notions of heaven and hell which were current in Jewish and Christian circles at the time of Muhammad are found in the holy book of Islam as well. The good will be taken to heaven, a pleasant place, where they will live eternally in the presence of God, while the evil will be driven into the eternal burning pit to suffer forever. This dualistic hereafter can be traced backward to origins in Persian religion, but it was extremely popular in the Mediterranean world in the middle of the first millennium C.E. Though there are no long lists of laws in the Qur'an, as there are in the biblical books of Exodus, Leviticus, and Deuteronomy, there are moral and legal statements scattered throughout the work. Adherence to these rules determines the status one has on the final day.

Finally, the notion of absolute monotheism is central to the Qur'an. It is believed that Abraham founded the faith that is now observed as Islam, though others before him had been allowed to understand that God alone was God. All forms of polytheism are considered heretical and outside the circle of the saved. Those people who believe in many gods need to be converted. The proper manner is to peacefully explain the truth of God to the unbelievers until they understand and accept the will of God. If they do not come to understand and prove to be violent toward the truth, they may be forcefully converted. Those who are "people of the Book," meaning Jews and Christians, are a harder problem. They have some of the truth, but not as full an understanding as do those with the Qur'an. Therefore, should they not be convinced through argumentation, they must be allowed to remain within the Islamic world and be allowed to continue to live with their own understanding. (True, not all Islamic societies have adhered to this norm in the Qur'an, but it has always remained the ideal).

Authority

Since the origin of the Qur'an is accepted in Islam to be the dictations of the angel Gabriel to Muhammad such that he both heard and saw the recitation, the divine character of the text is not questioned. There is one set text, and it has no variations; when variant texts were discovered, as when copied incorrectly, they were destroyed. The need for a single authoritative text, as mentioned before, reflects a knowledge of the Jewish and Christian problems of multiple editions and translations of their own sacred book(s). Once a single, completely consistent text of the Qur'an was accepted, the notion was adopted by certain circles of Judaism; it is from these Jews that the notion of an unchanging Hebrew text, which became the Massoretic Text of the Tanak, was developed. Islamic Qur'anic tradition early affected Jewish (and Christian) biblical traditions.

Once the text was set, it was also used to formulate legal and social regulations within Islamic societies. The study and formulation of law from the Qur'an is known as *sharia,* which has developed in a manner similar to the Jewish interpretation of biblical law in halakah. Any Muslim engaged in the law is expected to have memorized the Qur'an (as do most Muslim scholars in any of the traditional religious fields, as well as many lay Muslims in all Islamic traditions, much as it was common among Christians a century ago to have memorized their Bibles). There are various schools of sharia within Islam, so different areas of the Islamic world have different legal codes, though all are based on an authoritative study of the text of the Qur'an. It has been traditional in Islam to take the diversity of legal interpretation as something in which to take pride. Any legal decisions that might be incorporated from outside the tradition, as with modern attempts to impose universal human rights, must be understood as in conformity with the traditions of Qur'anic law.

For Muslims, the Qur'an is the word of God. This is the text that God has mercifully revealed to the believing community so that they might know how to live with God, in nature, and with each other. In Orthodox Judaism the Torah holds a similar position, but not exactly the same. In Christianity, except for some modern forms of fundamentalism, the Bible has never held as high a status; the word of God for Christians has traditionally been the person of Jesus as the risen Christ. The Bible has been read as pertaining to Christ and to God, but the exact wording was less important than the theology pertaining to the true word. Therefore, Christians have almost always treated the biblical text and its interpretation with less reverence (however high that reverence may have been) than have Muslims behaved toward the Qur'an.

Though most Muslims understand the Qur'an on a literal level, there have been a number of schools of interpretation. Those who read passages of the holy book through historical or philosophical traditions derived from classical Greek sources (which came to Islam early in its tradition by way of Byzantium Christianity) were nonetheless generally accepted as properly reading the sacred text. The natural sciences and social sciences were encouraged in the first millennium of Islam to the extent that Christians and Jews had to seek out Muslim scholars for the best in current education throughout the Middle Ages. These areas of study also were used in numerous traditions of Qur'anic understanding. Sufis are renowned for reading the Qur'an as a mystical text with hidden meanings. There are schools of students who seek to understand the text only in the manner of one teacher or school, and there have been Muslim scholars who used critical approaches to investigate the background and original meanings of the various texts. Islamic scholars, well before their Christian counterparts, made use of the different times in which the texts of their sacred book had been composed to describe various distinct and even inconsistent positions appearing in the text, though other scholars refuse to accept such scholarship or the existence of inconsistencies in the Qur'an.

In the same manner that many Christians read the Bible, most Muslims read the Qur'an as a single work, with a meaning that is to be taken as consistent throughout the surahs. Any text may be used with any other text without fear of its having a conflict. Also like many Christians, most Muslims do not read their holy text with a notion of the tradition that has gone into the current understanding of the "literal" text. However, it has long been the custom of Islamic scholars to recite the names of the earlier scholars in the line of tradition in which they speak (usually all the way back to Muhammad) to authenticate their own teaching.

Finally, there is *hadith. Hadith* is an oral tradition concerning Muhammad, early Islam, and interpretations of the Qur'an that was passed down orally, then written down, something like the Talmud in Judaism. This material is held in almost as high regard as the Qur'an but never can be used to contradict the clear sense of the holy book. Most of what is known about the life of Muhammad comes from the hadith and not from the Qur'an itself.

Questions for Reflection and Discussion
1. How might a Christian community use the Qur'an in understanding their own Bible?
2. What is the significance of Islamic belief that the Qur'an derives from the same heavenly source as the Jewish and Christian Bibles?
3. What is the difference (and what does it mean for individuals) between the biblical story of Adam and the Qur'anic story of Adam?
4. In what ways have the Christian and Muslim attempts to read their sacred texts been similar (or even influenced each other)?
5. In what ways might the Qur'an be considered interpretation of the Bible and of the Jewish and Christian traditions?

Bibliographical Note
There are several Qur'an translations/interpretations available in English; I used the standard, if somewhat awkward, Arthur J. Arberry translation, *The Koran Interpreted* (New York: Macmillan, 1955); a recent very readable Muslim translation, with its own essays and helps (from one particular Islamic circle) is Rashad Khalalfa, translator, *Quran: The Final Testament [Authorized English Edition]* (Tucson, Az.: Islamic Productions, 1989). Three books that might help put the Qur'an in perspective: Salim K. Haddad, *The Principles of Religion in the Qur'an and the Bible* (Pittsburgh: Dorrance Publishing, 1992), Fazlur Rahman, *Major Themes of the Qur'an* (Minneapolis: Bibliotheca Islamica, 1980), and Helmut Gätje, *The Qur'an and Its Exegesis: Selected Texts with Classical and Modern Muslim Interpretations*, translated by Alford T. Welch (Berkeley: University of California Press, 1971). Jane Dammen McAuliffe, "The Qur'anic Context of Muslim Biblical Scholarship," *Islam and Christian-Muslim Relations* 7 (1996), pp. 141-158, provides a succinct introduction to the Muslim reading of the Bible.

TWENTY BIBLE SCHOLARS
*E*VERYONE
SHOULD KNOW

THERE HAVE BEEN TENS OF THOUSANDS OF SIGNIFICANT BIBLI-
CAL scholars in the Jewish and Christian traditions. This session
looks at a mere twenty who have some right to be remembered by
those who read and interpret their Bibles. The selection is, by
choice, quite random, beginning chronologically with the Jewish
scholar Philo of Alexandria (d.ca. 50 C.E.), who most shaped the
allegorical interpretation of the Bible that became so dominant in
Christian thought, and ends with the Jewish philosopher Benedictus
(Baruch) de Spinoza (d. 1677), whose studies in philosophy and
Bible were a major foundation for modern Bible scholarship. Scholars, preachers, and laity from many Jewish and Christian traditions
of more recent times are worth investigating for their biblical contributions. The attempt here is merely to demonstrate the diversity of scholars and influential persons in Bible studies before the
burst of "modern" biblical research.

The format for the following is simple. For each entry there is
a paragraph of biographical material, a paragraph on the significance of the individual's biblical studies, and finally a suggested
bibliographical reference for each person listed. For a study group
session, each person might adopt one figure on which to do some
research and then present the findings to the class. However, these
short sketches will at least introduce these scholars' names.

Philo of Alexandria (±20 B.C.E.–±50 C.E.)

Philo was born into an influential Jewish family, probably in or near Alexandria, Egypt. Little is known of Philo's life, though his family was important, and we know more about several of his close relatives than about Philo himself. From his extensive writings it is clear that he was educated in Greek schools in Alexandria (a Greek city founded by Alexander the Great as a center for Greek culture that contained, by the first century B.C.E. a large Jewish population). Philo made a pilgrimage journey to Jerusalem sometime during his life. Though his actual position in the Jewish community of Alexandria is unknown, Philo was selected in 39 C.E. to be a member of a delegation sent to plead the case of the Jews living in Egypt before the Emperor Caligula in Rome. This suggests that he was known among his peers for more than his biblical and philosophical writings.

Philo was an extensive writer. His Bible was the Greek Jewish Bible used in the Jewish community in Alexandria. He produced a series of biblical commentaries, setting out the allegorical interpretations of numerous passages of scripture. Greek philosophical interpretations of classical Greek literature (particularly Homer and Hesiod) clearly were known to him. In a long work on Moses, Philo first describes Moses as a philosopher in the manner of Greek biographies of his time. Philo explained that Moses had been a giver of law, a priest, and a prophet, and insisted that Greek philosophers had attained their insights by reading Moses' Torah. Philosophical explanations of the Bible and of the Jews themselves in Philo's work show that he was writing for Jews who had become thoroughly accommodated to Greek culture. Central to Philo's understanding of the teachings of the Bible was the notion that the love between God and humans was the most important aspect to be learned from the texts, and he emphasized moral behavior as a way to God. Philo's works were preserved by Christians, who found his allegorical interpretations useful in their own faith, but were almost completely forgotten by later Jewish tradition until the nineteenth century.

Further reading: Samuel Sandmel, *Philo of Alexandria: An Introduction* (New York: Schocken Books, 1979). Dorothy Sly, *Philo's Alexandria* (New York: Routledge, 1995).

Johanan ben Zakkai (first century C.E.)

Though he is sometimes presented as the most influential Jewish figure of the time of Jesus, almost nothing is known of the life of

Johanan ben Zakkai. By tradition he was a pupil of the great Rabbi Hillel, but his own teachings became the basis for the Pharisaic Judaism that exists to this day. As a rabbi who taught at the Temple in Jerusalem, Johanan attempted to find a peaceful solution to the Jewish-Roman War (which ended in the burning of the Temple in 70 C.E.), but being unsuccessful, asked for permission from the Roman besiegers of Jerusalem to take his disciples from the city and was granted leave to do so. He established a rabbinic school in Jabneh, on the Mediterranean coast; there he continued to instruct his disciples until his death. He is remembered as a most humble, if brilliant, teacher of scripture and Jewish legal traditions. The Talmud cites Rabban Johanan ben Zakkai more frequently than any other rabbi.

While Johanan had an abiding interest in the Jewish mystical traditions and how they were found in the Bible, he is most remembered for keeping conventional rabbinic teachings alive during the demolition of much of Judaism in Judea during the Jewish-Roman War. The pattern of oral tradition that passed from teacher to pupil was maintained by him; he wrote no books. His method of dealing with any given passage of scripture was to extract it from its context (which was the standard method of reading biblical passages in both early Pharasaic Judaism and early Christianity) and then do intensive study of the words and their meaning for the passage itself. The object of biblical study was to derive from each passage its universal meaning. All passages, he believed, were capable of teaching Jew and Gentile alike how to live in the world.

Further reading: Jacob Neusner, *First Century Judaism in Crisis: Yohanan ben Zakkai and the Renaissance of Torah* (Nashville: Abingdon, 1975).

Origen (± 185–254)

Probably born in Alexandria, Origen was raised a Christian in a time of recurrent persecutions of the church in Egypt. In the persecutions of 202, when his father was slain, his attempt to become a martyr himself was foiled by his mother, who hid his clothes so he could not go out in public. Fascinated with the Bible and with the manner in which it was read, Origen wrote extensively about the various books of the Bible and how one might read them. Recognized for his brilliant insights, he was made the head of the Christian school in Alexandria, where his personal behavior and extensive knowledge of scripture and Christian exegesis made him famous throughout the Christian world. In 230 he was ordained, which angered the Bishop of Alexandria, who contested many of Origen's theological positions. Origen moved from Egypt to Caesarea (eastern coast of the Mediterranean) in 231, where he founded a school specializing in biblical exegesis. The pupils of this school became widely influential in biblical studies, both of orthodox Christians and various heretical Christian movements. Origen himself continued to teach until his death but was excommunicated only well after he was dead for several unorthodox theological positions .

Origen can honestly be called the most important early Christian Bible scholar. Only a few of his accomplishments may be mentioned here. His interest in the exact text of scripture led to his writing in ±245 the *Hexapla*, a parallel text of the Old Testament with six columns; the Hebrew text was in one column in Hebrew letters and beside it a column of Hebrew in Greek letters, then there were four columns, each with a different Greek translation of the Hebrew (some passages, where he could find them, had three more Greek translations). He produced an individual commentary on almost every book of the Bible, though only fragments are left of any of them (Origen having been declared excommunicate, his works were simply not copied in full; only those parts that later scholars felt were orthodox or useful were saved). From these fragments it is clear that Origen raised many of the questions that modern (or "postmodern") literary critics ask of texts. Origen explained that there were three levels of meaning for every scriptural passage: the Literal, the Moral, and the Allegorical. For Origen the most important of these was the allegorical, which bore the meaning of the text for all future generations (the least important for him was the literal). Origen's influence on later Christian exegesis in the church, East or West, can hardly be exaggerated.

Further reading: Origen, *On First Principles*, translated with introduction by G. W. Butterworth (Gloucester Mass.: Peter Smith, 1973).

Eusebius (±260–±340)

The Bishop of Caesarea from roughly 315, Eusebius was heavily influenced by the teachings of Origen, which he learned from one of Origen's students. He attempted to find middle ground between the orthodox theologians and the followers of Arius (who believed that Jesus was solely human and not divine), but to no avail. He is most remembered for having produced the first extensive history of the early church (in ten books written from ±303 to 323) and the *Life of Constantine,* which was a biography of the emperor who declared Christianity both legal and the state religion of the Roman Empire.

His renown in biblical study circles is based on a few, if important, works. In his history of the church he listed the scriptural books he considered authoritative; there, for the first time, the canon of the New Testament as it appears now was recorded. Probably the most important work for Bible scholars is Eusebius' *Onomasticon,* in which he attempted to correlate the place names in the Bible with the topography of the area of Judah and Israel as it was in his time. He also produced extensive commentaries on the Psalms and on Isaiah, as well as a collection of the prophecies in the Old Testament that foretold the life of Christ. His *Demonstration of the Gospel* set out, in twenty books, to prove the truth of Christianity by means of the Bible (which for him was still the Old Testament). His major method of interpreting texts was the allegorical method of Origen; however, he did have more interest in the historical value of the Bible than Origen had, and his central concern for the use of Old Testament passages as forerunners of the church brought proof-text investigations to a new level of scholarship.

Further reading: Robert M. Grant, *Eusebius as Church Historian* (Oxford: Oxford University Press, 1980).

John Chrysostom (±347–407)

John "the Golden Mouthed" was the Patriarch of Constantinople from 398 to 403, when he was driven from the office by church and royal opponents. A preacher by vocation, John was involved in both church and secular controversies for most of his life. He had a commitment to reforming the liturgy, and his work on the order of the Orthodox year remains the most widely followed liturgy among the Eastern churches to this day. He is credited with cleaning up the rampant corruption of the church hierarchy in Constantinople when he became Patriarch in 398. This would have made him enough enemies; but he also took to publicly denouncing the immoral behavior of the Empress Eudoria. The combination of ecclesiastical and royal enemies led to his trial on charges of heresy and slandering the empress (the heresy charges have been shown to have been invented by his enemies; the slander charges depend on whether publicly saying what appears to have been true was slander rather than just unwise politics), which resulted in his banishment from the capital. His banishment would eventually end in his death by exposure while being forced to travel in foul weather. A student of the Antioch School of biblical studies, John believed that all scripture should be read for its obvious meaning and should be used for the building up of the church. Therefore, it was deemed by him that the best use for the Bible was in preaching. Numerous of his sermons have been preserved. He often preached in a series that would cover the entire text of a given book of the Bible, explaining to the congregation what the text said and how they might incorporate it into their own lives. A different approach was to choose a single theme as the center of a sermon; he would then search out all references to that notion in the biblical texts. For John, the Bible had to be immediately clear to those for whom it was intended. So he believed that the allegorical interpretations of the Alexandrian School were not only false, but heretical. One might well say that for him the Christian congregation was the most important aspect of Bible study.

Further reading: J. D. N. Kelly, *Golden Mouth: The Story of John Chrysostom: Ascetic, Preacher, Bishop* (London: Duckworth, 1995).

Theodore of Mopsuestia (±350–428)

Not a great deal is known of the life of Theodore. He was Bishop of Mopsuestia, who wrote extensively on the Bible while corresponding regularly with priests and scholars throughout the Roman Empire. He had been a student of Diodore, who trained him in the Antioch School of Bible studies, and he was a friend to John Chrysostom. After his death he was condemned by the church for holding heretical views regarding the incarnation of Jesus.

Though Theodore left little immediate influence on biblical studies in the church, his surviving works have drawn much attention in the past hundred years. Here was a scholar who was a good millennium ahead of his time. Theodore insisted that the proper interpretation of a scriptural text had to begin with careful study of the language in which it was written and in the history which surrounded its composition. His work conveys a central concern for the original author of each piece of scripture and for the collector of each book of the Bible. He believed that the Old Testament had to be read on its own and not have the New Testament interpretations of earlier biblical texts be read into those historically earlier passages. He insisted that passages could not be taken out of context but always must be read in their larger context, that of the Bible book in which they are found. He held allegorical interpretations to be nonsense and of no value but believed that typology had a place, as long as one realized that such interpretation was merely a comparison and not an interpretation of the meaning of a text. Perhaps most noteworthy, however, of his many observations, was that the Greek translation of the Bible could not be taken as authoritative for the meaning of the Bible texts of the Old Testament; only reading the Hebrew "original" could give an accurate understanding.

Further reading: Dimitri Z. Zaharopoulos, *Theodore of Mopsuestia on the Bible: A Study of His Old Testament Exegesis* (New York: Paulist Press, 1989).

Jerome (342–420)

Eusebius Hieronymus was born in Strido on the Adriatic coast of Italy. A scholar of classical studies, he turned to biblical research upon having a dream in which he found himself accused of loving classical culture more than Christianity. He spent roughly five years as a hermit in the Syrian desert, during which time he learned Hebrew; this was uncommon for Christians at that time. Having been ordained in the East, he returned to Rome, where he served as Pope Damasus' secretary. He finally retired to Bethlehem, where he served as head of a monastery. He had an extensive correspondence with biblical scholars, friends, and antagonists. His opinions on almost every controversy of the church in his lifetime survive, since he felt compelled to join in all theological disputes. It is worth noting that Jerome valued the learning and company of women and included them in his circle of correspondents and friends.

The single most important scholarly production by Jerome was his translation of most of the Bible into standard Latin. The project was instigated by Pope Damasus so that the church in the West would have a Bible in its own language. This Bible, called the Vulgate, was translated for the most part by Jerome himself; it was to became the official Bible in the Roman Catholic Church for the following millennium-and-a-half. Jerome had suggested, without success, that the church accept as its Old Testament the Bible used at his time by the Jews with whom he studied. Jerome composed extensive commentaries on several books of the Bible, as well as introductions to each of the books of the Bible that he translated. He incorporated not only extensive Christian but also some Jewish scholarship into his work. For the benefit of Christians who could only read Latin, he translated some of the major Bible studies written by Greek-speaking Christian scholars into Latin for their use. Further reading: J. D. N. Kelly, *Jerome: His Life, Writings, and Controversies* (New York: Harper and Row, 1975).

Augustine (354–430)

Augustine, who was to become the most influential thinker in the Western world for fifteen hundred years, was born in Tagaste, North Africa. His mother attempted to raise her son as a Christian, but his own inclination was toward classical culture (his father was a pagan). He studied at the University of Carthage, moving from there to Rome to set up his own school of rhetoric. From 373 until 383 Augustine was an active member of the philosophical/religious movement of the Manichaeans. He left Manichaeanism when he found their philosophy incapable of answering some of his most fundamental questions, and upon hearing the sermons of the Christian Bishop Ambrose of Milan. Augustine had moved, with his mistress, from Rome to Milan when he found his students in Rome to be less than sterling. His conversion to Christianity came in reaction to a voice, which he took to be God's, telling him to read Romans 13:13. He was baptised in 387 and by 395 had become Bishop at Hippo in North Africa; this was a very fast promotion in the church at that time. (We do not know what happened to his mistress, who had given him a son.) His tenure as Bishop of Hippo was filled with writing on every conceivable topic related to the church. His theology was worked out to a large extent in polemical confrontation with a series of Christian movements that came to be called heretical (largely on his account). In all this, Augustine never let the parishes in his care take second place to his scholarship but took personal charge of his area. He died during the seige of Hippo by the Vandals.

Augustine's most abiding influence on the Bible comes from his theology rather than his Bible commentaries themselves. His position on "original sin" has meant that Christians have read "sin" into the Garden of Eden story to this day (it does not appear in the Hebrew—really, it doesn't; we owe this understanding to Augustine). He is the one who worked out the notion of justification by faith alone (in debate with Pelagius). The distinction between the world's logic and Christian faith was at the center of his "City of God," which combined classical history and the history in the Bible to explain how events on earth come to take place. Living in the Western church tradition, Augustine used allegorical interpretations for the Bible and tended to find clear references to Jesus in Old Testament texts such that the New Testament became the deciding influence on the meaning of all Bible texts.

Further reading: *Augustine: Confessions* (numerous editions). Peter Brown, *Augustine of Hippo: A Biography* (New York: Dorset Press, 1967).

Saadia Gaon (882–942)

Saadia was born in Pithom (Abu Suweir), Egypt, in an established Jewish community in the Cairo Caliphate. He does not appear to have come from a scholarly family, but he intensively studied the Torah, philosophy, and secular sciences in Egypt. In 922 he moved to Babylonia, since the center of Jewish scholarship was in Mesopotamia at that time. By 928 he had distinguished himself as a scholar and innovative exegete of scripture; for this reason he was appointed as the head of the Jewish Academy of Sura over the nominations of others who had studied in Babylonia longer and/ or came from influential families. His tenure as head of the academy was noted as a glorious period for Jewish studies. Saadia engaged actively in the debates between the traditional Jewish interpreters of scripture and the Jewish sectarians who rejected Talmudic writings.

Saadia is considered the first Jewish scholar to write books in the modern sense of the term. He produced a volume to describe in detail the manner by which the thirteen hermeneutical rules for interpreting scripture should be used. His extensive legal study produced not only responsa on particular cases in the Jewish community, but also a book describing the meaning and application of the 613 commandments of the Torah. His extensive work in Hebrew and Aramaic grammar led to a Jewish liturgy in Arabic as well as two Arabic translations of the Bible for those Jews in Mesopotamia who no longer could read Hebrew. One was a work of high scholarship, with commentaries; the other was a paraphrase for popular reading. Since Saadia believed God could be equated with the deity of classical philosophy as found in Aristotle and the Neo-Platonists, he would not describe (or translate) any description of God with human attributes. His extensive philosophical studies were put to use in his Bible commentaries, where he argued that revelation and logic were not at odds, such that the literal meaning of the

Bible should be read and understood as bearing logical content. His commentaries remained very influential in Jewish scholarship through the Medieval Period.

Further reading: Henry Malter, *Saadia Gaon: His Life and Works* (Philadelphia: Jewish Publication Society of America, 1921).

Rashi (1040–1105)

Solomon ben Isaac, undoubtedly the most influential Jewish exegete of the Medieval Period, was born in Troyes, France. He studied at Mainz and at Worms, becoming a master of Jewish tradition, knowing both conservative and liberal trends in interpreting the Torah. He returned to his hometown, where he became rabbi with his own academy. His writings were not only numerous but influential already in his own lifetime. He was an extensive writer of responsa (which he never collected or sorted, though later Jewish scholars edited his work). Rashi sought and taught peace among his congregants and a need for peace with the Christians among whom they lived as well; however, his community was caught up in the First Crusade of Christians to the Holy Land in 1095. Since it was common for crusaders to begin their march by forcefully converting Jews in their own countries as they went through, the Jewish communities of Mainz and Worms were both decimated through loss of those who converted to Christianity and those who died rather than convert. Rashi, who knew many of the victims from his school days, argued the lenient position after the forcefully converted Jews asked to return to their synagogues. It has been argued that the emotional strain of the crusades contributed to the death of this very pious scholar, who had urged his congregation to seek peace and love for everyone. The term Rashi was one of respect formed from his name: <u>Ra</u>bbi <u>Sh</u>lomo ben <u>I</u>saaq.

Rashi introduced into Jewish Bible commentary the notion that the literal meaning of the text was the one that needed to be understood. He rejected allegorical or philosophical readings of the Bible as being impositions on the text rather than content in the text. His extensive knowledge of Hebrew was brought to bear on the texts. He argued that first one had to have a clear understanding of the grammar; then one had to have a knowledge of the context of the passage in its wider biblical position. The use of passages taken out of context was not part of his method. Moreover, the relation of large passages of biblical books to other books, both as literature and as historical progression, was central to his research. The literal-historical tradition of biblical studies in the Western world (both Jewish and Christian) can be fairly ascribed as originating with the work of Rashi. An extensive author of responsa, Rashi was known for holding to conservative positions, not favoring innovation in legal interpretation.

Further reading: Esra Shereshevsky, *Rashi: The Man and His World* (New York: Sepher-Hermon Press, 1982). Chaim Pearl, *Rashi* (London: Peter Halban, 1988).

Bernard of Clairvaux (1090–1153)

Bernard was born into an influential family in Fontaines, France. He early in life decided that he wished to follow the vocation of a monk and entered the monastery at Citeaux in 1112. His devotion to the order and pious life led to his being sent to establish a monastery under his own care in 1115 at Clairvaux. As Abbot of Clairvaux, Bernard became perhaps the most influential monk in Western Christendom. He seems to have been at every major conference where church matters of major importance were discussed thoughout his life. He managed to back the winning side in the pope-antipope confrontation of 1130, which led to vast amounts of money, power, and privileges being extended to his order. Bernard was one of the instigators of the Second Crusade, 1147, which was a fiasco. Traditionally, it has been assumed that Bernard wrote the rules for the Knights Templars, one of two crusader-military Christian orders.

Bernard's contribution to biblical studies is not much appreciated these days. He was a master of the spiritual interpretation of scripture. His extensive commentaries on the Song of Songs were based in the common Christian notion that the poems described Christ and the Christian church as well as God and the soul of the Christian. A sense of the mystical union of the soul of the individual and the Holy Spirit runs through his understanding of the Bible. Since the biblical texts were inspired by the Holy Spirit, the reader whose soul was devout could understand the texts through the intervention of the Spirit. The use of spiritual interpretations of the biblical texts was declining when Bernard wrote; his commentaries both provide the last extensive spiritual interpretations and are examples of the best that this method of Bible understanding produced. The few attempts to revive the spiritual interpretation of scripture late in the Medieval Period were based on Bernard's work.

Further reading: Jean Leclercq, *Bernard of Clairvaux and the Cistercian Spirit* (Cistercian Study Series, 16; Kalamazoo, Michigan: Cistercian Publications, 1976). Brian P. McGuire, *The Difficult Saint: Bernard of Clairvaux and His Tradition* (Cistercian Study Series, 126; Kalamazoo, Michigan: Cistercian Publications, 1991).

Hugh of St. Victor (died 1142)

Very little is known of Hugh aside from his writings. Even his place of birth is debated, some claiming he came from the area of Iepre, Belgium, and others Saxony, Germany. The first certain date is that of his entry into the Augustianian monastery of Paris in 1115. He went to the monastery of St. Victor in 1118. His extensive writings dealt with theology, grammar, and geometry. From 1125 until his death, he taught at the St. Victor monastery where he was a lay religious, never becoming a monk himself.

Hugh was a mystic and believed that to understand the proper meaning of the allegorical interpretation of scripture one must first immerse oneself in Christian theology and read the texts of the Bible through the New Testament writings. However, his greatest contribution to biblical studies is not his mystical reading of the text, but his literal-historical approach. Influenced by Jewish scholars in the tradition of Rashi, his earlier contemporary, Hugh insisted that the literal reading of the Bible needed to be taken seriously, and to understand it one had to have a background in the sciences, history, and rational thought. One could not, he insisted, read the literal meaning of the Old Testament by reading the New Testament understanding of the earlier writings into it. So in his historical-literal commentaries he avoided typological interpretations or finding references to Jesus in Old Testament passages; however, he did insist in contrast to the Jewish scholars with whom he had studied that the prophecies were about Jesus. The clear literal understanding of the meaning of the Bible was necessary, he insisted, before one could turn to the other levels of meaning, about which he also wrote. He had a particular interest in the relation of the Bible to the liturgy. As the primary interpreter of the Jewish historical-literal method of interpretation to Christian tradition, Hugh of St. Victor stands at the beginning of the Christian Bible studies that would eventually become the Protestant interpretive method.

Further reading: Beryl Smalley, *The Study of the Bible in the Middle Ages* (Notre Dame: Notre Dame University, 1964), pp. 83-106.

Maimonides (1135–1204)

Moses ben Maimon was born in Cordova, Spain, in a period of Islamic rule during which the rulers favored an open society and generosity toward the Jewish population. He was trained in medicine and Talmudic studies. In 1149 the region was swept by an Islamic religious revival, causing the Jewish population either to convert or flee; Moses fled to Fez, Morocco, where Jews were still welcomed. The situation for Jews deteriorated steadily in Morocco, until in 1165 Maimonides fled again, this time to Cairo, by way of Palestine. A codifier of the Jewish legal texts, Maimonides has sometimes been referred to as the greatest Jewish thinker since Moses (the biblical one). Constantly writing even when in flight, Moses Maimonides produced no commentaries, but his understanding of how the tradition was passed on and what needed to be organized from the tradition made his work important. Once established in Egypt, Maimonides became the personal physician to the Caliph of Cairo, a position he held until his death.

Maimonides is most renowned in Jewish tradition for his *Mishna Torah*, a volume which codified all the laws that appear in the Torah. This work made reference to the legal texts much easier by arranging the material by subject. His *The Guide of the Perplexed* remains the first extensive reflection on reading the Bible through philosophical eyes, raising questions as to what can and what cannot be believed in the biblical text. *The Guide* posits that different people read the Bible in different manners, according to their level of comprehension. The literal meaning of the text, he argues, is meant for those with little capacity for reflective reasoning. Those who have some capacity to understand the philosophical tradition will be able to understand a different meaning than those who read the literal text, but those with extensive capacities to read with care and have high intelligence will see a totally different meaning in the texts. Those who truly know the meaning of the texts will not make fun of those who take the literal meaning as the only meaning. For Maimonides, those who sneer at others who do not see what they do in the text have both misunderstood the text and have demonstrated that they are ignorant of even what they claim to know. Much of Maimonides' philosophical work regarding the Bible deals with what one can or cannot know concerning God.

Further reading: Abraham Joshua Heschel, *Maimonides: A Biography* (New York: Farrar, Straus, Giroux, 1982).

Nahmanides (1194–1270)

Moses ben Nahman was born in the Jewish community of Gerona, Catalonia (Spain) where his Catalon name was Bonestrug da Porta. Trained both in Jewish Talmudic studies and in public administration, Moses worked for a succession of government officials. The rulers of Catalonia were Christian but found Nahmanides to be intelligent and loyal. King James I arranged for a disputation (a debate between two opinions) between a Dominican scholar and Moses ben Nahman on the subject "The Messiah." Unfortunately, Nahmanides won the debate handily, causing the Dominicans to condemn him. King James I defended him against their claims; this, however, led them to seek the aid of Pope Clement IV, who sided with the Dominicans. Under threat of excommunication (which was neither an idle nor a trivial matter in those days), the king had to banish Nahmanides. He fled to Palestine, where he lived his last days in the area of ancient Israel. Jewish scholars refer to him as Ramban [Rabbi Moses ben Nahman].

Nahmanides should be remembered for two reasons. First, he was a skilled kabbalist. Kabbalah is the major form of Jewish mysticism, and it has its own interpretation of scripture, based on a number of haggadic rules as well as some standardized allegorical traditions. In his kabbalistic treatise on Creation, he explained that the six days of creation in fact foretell the history of the world for six thousand years (a thousand years for each day). In fact, the entire Torah, he stated, told the future as well as the past. Interestingly, he used contemporary science and even Christian theology in his commentaries on the Hebrew texts. Second, he was renowned as a writer of responsa. His knowledge of the traditional interpretations of the Torah laws and his work in the secular administrations of the Christians who ruled over the Jewish community gave him a deep understanding about how to adapt the traditional ways to his current situation. His intention was to retain as much as possible of the traditions, as they had been handed down from the biblical period, in the use of the Jewish community of his own time.

Further reading: Isadore Twersky, *Rabbi Moses Nahmanides (Ramban): Explorations in His Religious and Literary Virtuosity* (Harvard University Center for Jewish Studies: Texts and Studies, 1; Cambridge, Massachusetts: Harvard University Press, 1983). David Novak, *The Theology of Nahmanides Systematically Presented* (Brown Judaic Studies, 271; Atlanta: Scholars Press, 1992).

Nicholas of Lyra (± 1270–1340)

Nicholas was born in Lyre, Normandy (France). He became a Dominican friar. As a student he studied at the University of Paris, becoming a professor at the Sorbonne, where he taught until his death. Unhappy with the traditional Christian teachings regarding the interpretation of scripture, he studied the Jewish commentators who worked in the tradition of Rashi. Among his many biblical writings are those concerned with the liturgy of the eucharist (Lord's supper).

Influenced by Rashi, Nicholas turned his attention away from allegorical interpretations of scripture and concentrated on the literal and historical meaning of the biblical texts as they appear, and not as the theological traditions had read them. He had learned Hebrew from Jewish scholars so that he could read the Old Testament in its original language (though he never did learn Greek for the New Testament). His most influential work was his commentary on the entire Bible using only the literal level of interpretation, which was the first complete Bible commentary in a single reference work. His own research on the Old Testament had no Christian parallels or forerunners but was of extensive importance for those Christians who came to interpret the Bible in its literal meaning, including all branches of the Reformation.

Further reading: Herman Hailperin, *Rashi and the Christian Scholars* (Pittsburgh: University of Pittsburgh Press, 1963), pp. 135-246.

Christine de Pizan (± 1364–± 1431)

Born in Venice, Italy, Christine moved as child to France with her father, who served in the court of Charles V. She was educated in classical literature and the arts before she was married at the age of fifteen; her husband died ten years later, leaving her with three children and no means of support. She was determined to make her own living and did so by writing on contract. During her lifetime, Christine was renowned for her skill as an author and poet, such that many of her works survive, including a biography of Charles V intended to display proper behavior for rulers. While she presented the ten years of her own marriage as exceptionally happy, she made extensive comments on the evils most men perpetrate on women. She had an eye for the literary degradation of women, writing one entire work in protest of the popular but unrealistic Medieval portrayals of women written by male authors of romances. Currently, the most famous of her works is her *City of*

Women, which was published after her death, presenting a woman's vision of the world decidedly at odds with that presented in the contemporary male-composed manuscripts. In 1415 she retired to the Dominican convent at Poissy, where she died.

Her contributions to biblical studies consist of a series of publications on the moral meaning of scripture adapted for the use of women (and men) in her own age. Using both the tradition of moral interpretation of the Bible and her own understanding of the texts, Christine set out advice on selected topics concerning proper behavior for young ladies. In her various writings she sets forth her own positions concerning women in the Bible, which were not the standard church teachings. She explains that Eve was not at fault for the fall, since she had been lied to, seduced, and abandoned by the serpent (like, she says, too many young women by men in her own time); at the same time, she argues, Adam had no excuse for his taking the forbidden fruit. She also made the observation that people should notice that the scriptures showed all men abandoning Jesus when the going became rough, but there is not one instance of a woman abandoning the Lord; Christine suggested that there was much to learn from just that fact alone.

Further reading: Enid McLeod, *The Order of the Rose: The Life and Ideas of Christine de Pizan* (Totowa, N. J.: Rowan and Littlefield, 1976). Charity Cannon Willard, *Christine de Pizan: Her Life and Works* (New York: Persea Books, 1984).

Martin Luther (1483–1546)

Martin Luther was born in Mansfield, Saxony (Germany), in a mining district. Due to a vow made to God while frightened during a thunderstorm, Martin entered the Augustinian monastery at Erfurt in 1505. In two years he was ordained as a priest, while he continued his studies in theology and scripture, leading to a professorship at the University of Wittenberg in 1511. In reaction to the abuse of the papal office, Luther wrote his "95 Theses," which were topics on which he wished to debate certain current positions of the Catholic Church. Luther broke with Rome and declared that Christians should be directed by no human, but only by scripture. From biblical examples, he determined that clergy should be married and proceeded to marry and raise a large family. Confrontations with Rome led to the break of several areas within Germany from the Catholic Church and the rise of what has come to be known as Lutheranism.

Luther's studies of the Bible influenced more than just Lutherans or Bible scholars. Luther, believing that all Christians needed to read and understand the Bible on their own, translated the entire Bible into German. Not only did this give the German people a Bible they could read, but it presented them with a common German language, something that the various city-states had not had before. Luther believed that early Christians had used the Bible of the Jews as their own Bible; therefore, he insisted that the Christian Old Testament should be the same as the Jewish Bible that he knew in his own time. To this end, he removed those works he considered apocryphal and added them as an appendix to his Bible. This became the canon of the Protestant Bible. He wrote extensive commentaries on numerous books of both the Old and New Testaments, working from the original languages of Hebrew and Greek, both of which he read. His understanding of the texts was heavily influenced by Augustinian theology. The distinction made by Paul, as understood by Augustine, between the Law of the Old Testament and the Gospel of the New Testament became a cornerstone of Luther's theology and was the lens through which he read the entire Bible. The New Testament proclamation of Jesus as the Christ was central to his understanding of the texts of the Old Testament. Moreover, he believed, from his reading of Paul's letter to the Romans, that the legal materials of the Old Testament had ceased to be authoritative, and he therefore dismissed the Law from a place of any importance in his theology of the salvation of the Christian. Any book that did not stress the importance of grace over law, he dismissed as useless; so both Revelation and (especially) James were taken by him to be expendable, if not downright evil.

Further reading: Roland H. Bainton, *Here I Stand: A Life of Martin Luther* (New York: New American Library, 1950). Heiko A. Oberman, *Luther: Man between God and the Devil* (New Haven: Yale University Press, 1989).

Argula von Grumbach (1492–1563+)

Argula was probably born in Beratzhausen, Germany, the ancestral home of her impoverished, if formerly noble family, the Hohenstaufens. She was trained to be a maid-in-waiting, for which she was instructed in reading and writing. Married to a minor government official, she might have spent the rest of her life as a housewife, content to read the German translation of the Bible that had been given her. However, when the University of Ingolstadt in 1523 removed a junior faculty member for holding views derived from Luther, Argula came to his defense. She wrote a letter to the University and another to the government demanding that the scholar be reinstated, and she even challenged them all to a debate. She was invited to speak at the Diet at Nürnberg that same year and distinguished herself by defending Luther on biblical grounds. This, however, led to the dismissal of her husband from his position, which he took out on her in physical abuse. She refused to recant her defense of Luther, though she herself maintained loyalty to the Catholic Church; she insisted that Luther was both correct and a good Catholic. She kept up a correspondence with Luther (which is now lost), and her writings were among the most popular of the early Reformation, printed through several editions. She, however, dropped out of sight so that the date and circumstances of her death are unknown.

Argula took Luther's call for Bible study by all Christians seriously. If every Christian could read the Bible for its clear sense and understand what it meant for the current world, then that included women as well as men. In spite of vitriolic attacks on her as a woman attempting to do theological work, she maintained that anyone could, and should, use the Bible to correct the errors of the modern world. Lutherans of the time eagerly promoted her works that insisted that women were as capable as any Christian to read and use the Bible and that women's voices needed to be heard; Catholics of the time dismissed her as evil. Aside from her recognition as a woman who could properly use the Bible, she was also recognized for using biblical passages to confront both civil and church authorities on questions of corruption and oppression. For Argula the Bible was the sole basis on which to ground politics, morals, and law; all regulations and officials who ignored the dictates of the Bible for a just and equitable society should be removed. With the Protestant reformers, Argula argued that the final and exclusive authority for a Christian world was the Bible and no other.

Further reading: Peter Matheson, editor, *Argula von Grumbach: A Woman's Voice in the Reformation* (Edinburgh: T. & T. Clark, 1995). Roland Bainton, *Women of the Reformation in Germany and Italy* (Boston: Beacon Press, 1971), pp. 97-109.

John Calvin (1509–1564)

Jean Calvin was born in Noyon, Picardy, France. As a young man he was a humanist typical of his age who studied at Orleans and Bourges to become a lawyer. However, his attention turned to the current state of the church in Europe, such that he determined that the corruption of the Christian world needed to be cleared away. In 1533 he broke with Rome, aligning himself with the Reformed Movement already embattled in Switzerland's politics and state confrontation with the Catholic Church. Calvin believed the church could return to the original organization of the church as it was in its pure state at the time of Acts. His most famous work is *The Institutes*, a treatise on how to organize the church in the world. It was first printed in 1536; he re-edited it several times before it reached its final form in 1559. It remains the foundational text for Reformed churches throughout the world. In 1555 Calvin became the head of the city of Geneva, a position he would hold until his death. In an attempt to create the perfect Christian community, Calvin ruled with a strict control of the lives of the citizens, punishing those who disrupted the city, expelling those who broke major regulations, and executing heretics. In this he was evenhanded; his own family was not spared from having to obey the rules or be banished. Needless to say, he was both loved and hated by the populace.

Calvin is most remembered for reading the Bible so as to create a Christian world that could function in the sixteenth century. He wrote commentaries on almost all the books of the Bible with the intention of making the texts both understandable to the reader and useful for the "modern" community. There is a clear concern for the community as well as the individual. Most original to Calvin's biblical research among the Protestants, however, is his insistence that the Old Covenant was not superseded by the New Convenant; that is, God's promise to the Jews remains valid; the church has only joined them, not supplanted them. In this vein, Calvin stressed the need to take the legal texts of the Torah seriously and adapted them to meet the needs of his own world; only those regulations that were clearly changed in the New Testament could be understood as having ceased to be required. The books of the Old Testament, while they might be read with an understanding of the New Testament use of them, still needed to be read on their own. As for the New Testament, he argued that all the books of the canon were of equal value.

Further reading: George Richard Potter, *John Calvin* (New York: St. Martin's Press, 1983). Alister E. McGrath, *A Life of John Calvin: A Study in the Shaping of Western Culture* (Oxford: Basil Blackwell, 1990).

Benedictus de Spinoza (1632–1677)

Born in Amsterdam, Baruch Spinoza was raised in the well-established Sephardic (Spanish) Jewish community in the Netherlands. He was trained in traditional Jewish studies but also had a natural interest in contemporary philosophy. In 1656 he and two Christians publicly questioned the received tradition that Moses had written the Torah (Baruch also went on to question the story of Adam as the first man and whether the Torah was superior to Natural Law as a source for understanding the world). While the other two withdrew their questions under pressure from the Christian community, Spinoza insisted to the Jewish community that it was a legitimate question to ask and discuss; on July 27, 1656, Baruch Spinoza was excommunicated from the Jewish community. He then studied philosophy at the University of Leiden and took up lens-grinding to make a living. He moved to The Hague, where he became a regular member of a group of liberal Protestants who discussed biblical, theological, and philosophical topics. Asked to become a professor, he declined, saying that lens-grinding was a fulfilling occupation and it allowed him time to think. Though he changed his name to Benedictus de Spinoza and was popular among certain circles of Protestant scholars, he never became a member of the Dutch church.

The modern world of biblical studies is often dated to the publication of Spinoza's *Tractatus Theologico-Politicus* in 1670. Spinoza accepted the Protestant belief that all could read the Bible on their own and thereby understand what it means. To do this, one needed to read the literal meaning of the text in a rational manner. Since he believed that the Bible was to be read like any other book, he held that the authors of the books of the Bible needed to be known and studied. For him, the author of the current Bible from Genesis through Kings (Hebrew order, so without Ruth) was Ezra, but he believed that work contained earlier writings by others (including, for example, the sections of the Torah that he was certain Moses did write). Other books he tended to date from the fifth to the first centuries B.C.E. His three-fold method for approaching the study of individual biblical books is still followed in critical scholarship: 1) analyze the Hebrew language of the book, 2) study each book on its own, and 3) determine the origins, the transmission, and the canonization of each book. Spinoza firmly believed that the prophets did speak the word of God, but that it need not be taken literally rather than as a teaching aid; he also believed that parts of the

Bible we simply do not understand because the context in which it was written has been lost to us. Spinoza did think the current canon needed some changes. Regarding the Jewish Bible, he believed that Chronicles should have been left out, but that the Wisdom of Solomon and the book of Tobit should have been included. He blamed the Pharisees, who had made the decisions about the extent of the canon, for having made these bad choices.

Further reading: Alan Dongan, *Spinoza* (Chicago: University of Chicago, 1988).

Questions for Reflection and Discussion

1. Can anyone think of any other Bible scholars from the "premodern" (up to Spinoza) period who have had a major influence on the individual's or congregation's reading of the Bible? Who are the modern Bible interpretors who have most influenced you?

2. For any of the persons dealt with here, what, if any, of their work would you consider to be still valuable in your own Bible study or in that of your congregation?

3. What can be said about the interaction of Jews and Christians in the history of the interpretation of scripture?

4. What are the advantages or disadvantages of having every member of the church or synagogue read the meaning of the Bible on his or her own, as opposed to having an authority explain the meaning of the texts?

5. What are your own methods of interpreting the Bible texts?